THE CATHOLIC UNIVERSITY OF AMERICA
CANON LAW STUDIES
Number 85

THE DEFENSOR VINCULI

HIS RIGHTS AND DUTIES

A DISSERTATION

Submitted to the Faculty of Canon Law of the Catholic University of America in Partial Fulfillment of the Requirements for the Degree of

DOCTOR OF CANON LAW

BY

REV. JOHN LEO DOLAN, J.C.L.,
Priest of the Archdiocese of New York

THE CATHOLIC UNIVERSITY OF AMERICA
WASHINGTON, D. C.
1934

Nihil Obstat:

Valentinus T. Schaaf, O.F.M., J.C.D.,
Censor Deputatus.

Washingtonii, D. C., die 11 Maii, 1934.

Imprimatur:

Patritius Cardinalis Hayes,
Archiepiscopus Neo Eboracensis.

Neo Eboraci, die 15 Maii, 1934.

Printed by
The Paulist Press
New York, N. Y.

THE DEFENSOR VINCULI

HIS RIGHTS AND DUTIES

TABLE OF CONTENTS

CHAPTER I

PAGE

THE HISTORICAL BACKGROUND OF THE OFFICE OF *DEFENSOR VINCULI* 1

ART. I. PRE-BENEDICTINE DEFENSE OF THE MARRIAGE BOND 2

ART. II. POSSIBLE REMOTE ORIGINS OF THE OFFICE 5

1. A Suggestion of Hostiensis 5
2. Possible Origin in Duties Formerly Attached to the Office of the Promotor of Justice 9

ART. III. THE CONDITIONS THAT IMPELLED THE POPE TO INSTITUTE THE OFFICE OF *Denfensor Vinculi* 14

CHAPTER II

SOME GENERAL NOTIONS IN CONNECTION WITH THE OFFICE OF *DEFENSOR VINCULI* 17

ART. I. THE APPOINTMENT OF THE *Defensor Vinculi* 17

ART. II. THE TENURE OF OFFICE OF THE *Defensor Vinculi* 25

ART. III. PERSONAL REQUIREMENTS IN THE INCUMBENT 28

ART. IV. PRELIMINARY FORMALITIES 33

ART. V. THE CAUSES IN WHICH THE *Defensor Vinculi* MUST INTERVENE 35

CHAPTER III

PAGE

THE *DEFENSOR VINCULI* IN THE FIRST OR PROBATORY PERIOD OF THE TRIAL 41

General Remarks

ART. I. THE PRESENCE REQUIRED ON THE PART OF THE *Defensor Vinculi* 41

ART. II. THE RIGHT OF THE *Defensor Vinculi* TO SEE THE *Acta* OF THE TRIAL 44

ART. III. THE *Defensor Vinculi* IN THE PRELIMINARY STAGES OF THE TRIAL 46

ART. IV. THE *Defensor Vinculi* IN THE PRELIMINARY INVESTIGATION THAT MUST PRECEDE THE OPENING OF THE TRIAL WHEN COMPETENCE IS DERIVED FROM *quasi-domicile* 50

ART. V. THE *Defensor Vinculi* IN THE PROBATORY SESSIONS OF THE TRIAL 56

A. His Rights in the Calling of Witnesses 56

B. The Order in Which the Witnesses Are to be Heard 60

C. Special Rights Enjoyed by the *Defensor Vinculi* in the Calling of Witnesses 61

ART. VI. THE *Defensor Vinculi* IN THE EXAMINATION OF PARTIES AND WITNESSES 63

ART. VII. THE *Defensor Vinculi* AND THE WRITTEN DEPOSITIONS OF PARTIES AND WITNESSES 66

ART. VIII. THE *Defensor Vinculi* AND THE EXPERTS (PERITI) IN THE TRIAL 71

ART. IX. THE DUTIES OF THE *Defensor Vinculi* IN CONNECTION WITH ROGATORY COMMISSIONS 73

PAGE

Art. X. The Declaration of Contempt and Its Reference to the *Defensor Vinculi* 77

Art. XI. The Duty of the *Defensor Vinculi* with Regard to Documents Entered in the Trial 78

Art. XII. The *Defensor Vinculi* and the Suppletory Oath 79

Art. XIII. The Duty of the *Defensor Vinculi* with Reference to Interpreters 80

Art. XIV. The *Defensor Vinculi* and Ocular Inspection (*Accessus Judicialis*) 80

Art. XV. Two Minor Applications of the Rights of the *Defensor Vinculi* to the Law of the Trial 82

CHAPTER IV

THE *DEFENSOR VINCULI* IN THE REMAINING STAGES OF THE TRIAL 84

Art. I. The *Conclusio in Causa* and *Publicatio Processus* 84

Art. II. The Summing Up (*Discussio Causae*) 86

Art. III. The *Defensor Vinculi* and the Final Sentence 91

Art. IV. The *Defensor Vinculi* in the Incidental Trial 93

CHAPTER V

THE *DEFENSOR VINCULI* IN APPEAL 99

Art. I. Definitions 99

Art. II. The *Defensor Vinculi* and His Obligation to Appeal from a Sentence for Nullity 101

Art. III. Some Special Applications of the Duty of the *Defensor Vinculi* in Connection with Appeals 110

PAGE

Art. IV. The Prosecution of the Appeal of the *Defensor Vinculi* 114

Art. V. The Meaning of the Phrase "Two Comformable Sentences" in the Legislation Dealing with the *Defensor Vinculi* 116

Art. VI. The *Defensor Vinculi* and the Complaint of Nullity (*Querela Nullitatis*) 119

Art. VII. Some Remarks on the Procedure of Appeal with Reference to the *Defensor Vinculi* 121

FINAL CONCLUSIONS 124

APPENDIX I. The *Defensor Vinculi* in the Cases Ruled by Canon 1990 126

APPENDIX II. The *Defensor Vinculi* in the *Ratum et Non Consummatum* Process 130

BIBLIOGRAPHY 143

INDEX 147

BIOGRAPHICAL NOTE 149

CANON LAW STUDIES 151

FOREWORD

THE name of Pope Benedict XIV occupies no small place in the history of Canon Law. He appears upon its pages in a double guise for, in them, he is disclosed both as a simple canonist expounding the law and as Pope—the maker of laws. Prosper de Lambertini was well fitted to occupy the highest post in Christendom, for he brought to the Chair of Peter a well trained mind, the result of twenty years of experience as Secretary of the Congregation of the Council.

This was the Pope who gave to the Church the laws which regulate all trials in which the validity of a marriage is involved. These laws were promulgated in the now celebrated Constitution "*Dei Miseratione*" of November 3, 1741.[1]

One of the salient features of these laws was an innovation—a new office, that of the "*Matrimoniorum Defensor,*" [2] now known as the "*Defensor Vinculi Matrimonialis,*" [3] or simply as the "*Defensor Vinculi.*" [4]

It is this office, that of the *Defensor Vinculi Matrimonialis,* which is the subject of this study. The scope of the study, however, will be limited to an examination of the rights and duties of the *Defensor Vinculi* in those matrimonial trials in which his intervention is demanded by law. It will not therefore concern itself expressly with the duties of the *Defensor Sacrae Ordinationis,* for the simple reason that the difference between the duties of the *Defensor Vinculi* in these two capacities is very slight.[5]

It is the duty of the *Defensor Vinculi Matrimonialis* to defend all marriages when their validity is called into question before the ecclesiastical court,[6] and consequently it is evident that he fills an important part in the matrimonial legislation introduced by Benedict XIV.

[1] *Fontes,* n. 318.

[2] *Dei Miseratione,* n. 5.

[3] Canon 1967.

[4] Canons 1586, 1588, 1589, 1968, 1969, 1990, 1991, 1992.

[5] Canon 1996.

[6] Benedict XIV, const., *Dei Miseratione,* n. 6—*Fontes,* n. 318.

The purpose of the legislation of Benedict XIV was to prevent the acquisition of declarations of nullity from the Church courts through fraud, an abuse quite prevalent in the early eighteenth century.[7]

The matrimonial laws of Benedict XIV, drawn up for the purpose of extirpating this abuse, did not achieve final success without some opposition. In the year 1743, almost two full years after the issuance of the constitution *"Dei Miseratione,"* we find the Pope still protesting to the Bishops of Poland about abuses of this type still prevalent in that country.[8]

Success, however, finally rewarded the persistent efforts of the Pontiff, for in the year 1746, we find him writing the following in reference to his celebrated constitution *"Dei Miseratione":*

> Cuius quidem Constitutionis utilitas, Deo favente, ad hunc diem aperte comprobatur: quum ex eo tempore, neque tot Causae super praetensa Matrimoniorum nullitate in Tribunalibus pendeat; nec tam frequenter, ut antea, Nobis exhibeantur preces pro obtinendis dispensationibus super Matrimonio rato, et non consummato:[9]

In fact so well pleased was the Pope with the effectiveness of the *Defensor Vinculi Matrimonialis* that he created a like office for the protection of religious profession from dishonest attack. The new official bore the name of *Defensor Professionis Religiosae,* and his office was similar in both rights and obligations to that of the *Defensor Vinculi Matrimonialis.*[10]

The *Defensor Vinculi* is an official of the Diocesan Curia,[11] constituted by legitimate authority, to defend *ex officio* and in accordance with the requirements of the Code of Canon Law, the validity of all marriages called into question before the ecclesiastical court.[12]

[7] Benedict XIV, const., *Dei Miseratione,* nn. 1, 2—*Fontes,* n. 318.

[8] Benedict XIV, encycl., *Nimiam Licentiam,* May 18, 1747—*Fontes,* n. 337.

[9] Benedict XIV, const., *Si Datam,* March 4, 1748—*Fontes,* n. 385.

[10] Const., *Si Datam,* n. 11.

[11] Canon 363, § 2.

[12] Canon 1586; Wernz-Vidal, *Jus Canonicum,* VI, n. 111; Noval, *De Processibus,* p. 79.

In general the duty of the *Defensor Vinculi* may be said to consist of the obligation to intervene in all matrimonial trials where the validity or the nullity of a marriage is contested before a legitimately constituted Ecclesiastical Judge. This duty implies that the *Defensor Vinculi* must be cited to attend all judicial sessions, that he should be present at the examination of the *parties* to the trial, and of all witnesses. He also has the duty to sustain the validity of the contested marriage both orally and in writing before the Court.[13]

The law itself indicates the importance of the role that this official plays in the matrimonial trial by its provision nullifying the *acta* of those trials requiring the presence of the *Defensor Vinculi,* in which not being cited, he has failed also to intervene.[14]

It will be the purpose of this study to examine the duties of the *Defensor Vinculi,* both in the light of the present law of the Code, and also in the light of the Pre-Code law whenever it is necessary or helpful to do so.

The Constitution, "*Dei Miseratione,*" is of course an important source of Pre-Code law,[15] but in addition to the "*Dei Miseratione*" several other instructions were issued by the Holy See in connection with the procedure of the Matrimonial trial. Of these two are of the greatest importance, both because they became the basis of the future instructions, and because they are actually official commentaries on the law of the "*Dei Miseratione*" as well.

Chronologically the first of these instructions is the one issued by the Sacred Congregation of the Council under the date of the twenty-second of August, 1840.[16]

The second instruction issued in the year 1883, is a rather detailed instruction on the matrimonial trial. It was issued by the Sacred Congregation of the Holy Office to the Oriental Bishops, and was also despatched with but few minor changes by the Sacred Con-

[13] Canon 1586; Benedict XIV, const., *Dei Miseratione,* n. 6—*Fontes,* n. 318.

[14] Canon 1587, § 1; Benedict XIV, const., *Dei Miseratione,* n. 7—*Fontes,* n. 318.

[15] *Fontes,* n. 318.

[16] *Fontes,* n. 4069.

gregation of the Propaganda to the Bishops of the United States in the same year.[17]

There is another important source of law in force today that involves the *Defensor Vinculi.* It is the Instruction, "*Catholica Doctrina,*" of the Sacred Congregation of the Sacraments, issued under the date of May 7, 1923, with its accompanying rules and norms that regulate the investigation that must be made before a dispensation from an unconsummated marriage is granted by the Holy Father.[18]

The writer wishes at this point to express his gratitude to all those who have assisted him in the writing of this monograph. He is especially indebted to the members of the Faculty of Canon Law of the Catholic University for their valuable assistance and wise direction in the preparation of this study.

[17] *Fontes,* n. 1076.

[18] *AAS* XV (1923), 397; also the Instr., *S. C. de Sacram.*, March 27, 1929—*AAS* XXI (1929), 490.

CHAPTER I

THE HISTORICAL BACKGROUND OF THE OFFICE OF THE *DEFENSOR VINCULI*

THE actual origin of the office of *Defensor Vinculi* is shrouded neither in mystery nor in dim antiquity, since it is an office of comparatively recent origin owing its foundation to Pope Benedict XIV who instituted the office on November 3, 1741.[1]

No evidence is to be found in Roman Law of any office bearing the slightest resemblance to the office of the present day *Defensor Vinculi*. Roman Law had its "*defensores*," but they resemble the *Defensor Vinculi* in name alone.[2]

Nor is this fact surprising, when it is considered that the very reason for the existence of the office of *Defensor Vinculi* is the Christian teaching that Matrimony is a sacrament, sacred and indissoluble—a truth well expressed by Pope Benedict XIV himself in the following words:

> Matrimonii perpetuum indissolubilemque nexum, cuius firmitatem ab Adamo tanto ante pronuntiatam Christus Dominus, et his verbis, *quod Deus coniunxit, homo non separet*, confirmare, et Evangelica gratia, unde magnum in Ecclesia Sacramentum est, . . .[3]
> Siquidem Matrimonii foedus a Deo institutum, quod, . . . perpetuum, et indissolubile esse convenit; . . .[4]

It was because of this teaching of Holy Mother Church that Pope Benedict formulated legislation to curb abuses prevalent at the time, arising from the careless handling of matrimonial trials.

[1] Benedict XIV, const., *Dei Miseratione—Fontes,* n. 318; Joyce, *Christian Marriage,* p. 400.

[2] D. III, *de procuratoribus et defensoribus.*

[3] Benedict XIV, encycl., *Matrimonii,* April 11, 1741—*Fontes,* n. 307.

[4] Benedict XIV, const., *Dei Miseratione,* November 3, 1741—*Fontes,* n. 318.

The heart of this remedial legislation of Pope Benedict XIV is the office of the *Defensor Vinculi,* the subject of this study.

Article I

Pre-Benedictine Defense of the Marriage Bond

While it is beyond the realm of controversy that Benedict XIV created the office of *Defensor Vinculi,* yet the sudden appearance of this office in such complete and perfect form as that which it enjoyed from the very beginning impels one to look further back in history for the more remote origins of the office.

Was there an office previous to the time of Benedict XIV charged with the defense of the marriage bond? The answer to this question is an emphatic no. In the law anterior to the legislation of Benedict XIV there is to be found no provision for an officer of the Curia empowered to act after the manner of the Benedictine *Defensor Vinculi.* Neither the inquisitorial process of Innocent III [5] nor the summary process of Clement V [6] made any provision for this type of *ex officio* protection of marriage.

The general tenor of the Constitution "*Dei Miseratione*" in which the office is described for the first time, points to the institution of a new office, because of the complete and thorough treatment which it receives.

The office is described in full detail, its duties accurately outlined, and its title carefully given, ". . . *persona* . . . *quae Matrimoniorum Defensor nominabitur* . . ."; all in such fashion as to indicate the complete consideration given to a new and carefully devised piece of legislation.[7]

In laying down these rules the Pope referred to no law or regulation then in force, and indeed before the year 1741, no Pope or Council can be found making reference to an official whose duty was to defend the sacrament of Marriage when its validity was attacked in court.

[5] C. 24, X, *de accusationibus, inquisitionibus, et denunciationibus,* V, 1.

[6] C. 2, *de iudiciis,* II, 1, in Clem.

[7] Benedict XIV, const., *Dei Miseratione,* n. 5—*Fontes,* n. 318.

There can be little doubt that the office of *Defensor Vinculi* was solely the creation of Pope Benedict XIV when the question is considered in the light of the conditions that lead to the institution of the office, which will be adequately discussed later in the development of this study.

The primitive Church was preoccupied with the problem of divorce in the true sense of the word, the official dissolution of a valid marriage. Divorce in this sense is not to be confused with a declaration of nullity, which merely declares that a marriage is not and has never been valid.

The silence of history with regard to this latter type of dissolution of marriage is no indication that there were no such cases during those early days.[8]

It is merely an indication that the energies of the Bishops of those times were taken up with the larger problem of divorce in the strict sense, the official dissolution of a valid marriage. It was only natural therefore that the need for an official such as the *Defensor Vinculi* did not arise, and hence we find no mention of an office even similar in nature.

These early converts entered the Church with the Jewish and Pagan ideas of divorce in the strict sense. The Church had to direct her efforts against this practice so completely at variance with the Christian teaching on the permanence and indissolubility of marriage. The congregations in the early Church were also small in numbers and the Bishop, intimately acquainted with the affairs of his flock, was often consulted by the faithful even before entering into marriage.[9] Such conditions were practically ideal, and very little trouble with regard to invalid marriages could possibly arise, hence there would be little reason for the existence of an official similar to the *Defensor Vinculi.*

With the grant of civil freedom to the Church, the numbers of the faithful grew, and with the increase came new difficulties.

In the year 506 the Council of Agde is found cutting off from the communion of the faithful those who brought marriage cases involv-

[8] Wernz-Vidal, *Jus Canonicum,* V, p. 825.

[9] Letter of St. Ignatius to Polycarp, Chap. V—*MPG,* V, 723.

ing divorce or separation before any officials other than the bishops of the province.[10]

This was an indication of a change in conditions, and the consequent beginning of a different period, bringing with it new troubles that were in time to give rise to the situation calling for specific remedies.

Up to the eighth century cases of annulment were infrequent,[11] and hence lack of legislation on the point is but natural. This may be attributed to the small number of invalidating impediments in force at the time.[12]

With the eighth century these impediments began to increase, and with this increase naturally came an increase in the number of trials in which a declaration of nullity was sought.

The Church ever mindful of the sanctity and perpetuity of marriage always sought to protect a valid marriage. She therefore determined not only those who could attack the validity of a marriage, but also those who could testify against it as well.[13]

The common law of the Church demanded that the nullity of the marriage be proven by at least two witnesses who were above all suspicion.[14] Marriage always enjoyed a favorable presumption before the law, and as long as the marriage was not proven null, the judge pronounced in favor of the validity of the marriage.[15]

The canonical writers of the time discussed at great length, the degree of certainty that the proofs ought to give in order that the marriage might be declared null. They were chiefly concerned, as was the law itself, with the prevention of collusion between the parties themselves and their adherents.[16]

As long as one of the parties defended the marriage these men seemed to be satisfied that the marriage was sufficiently protected.

[10] C. XXV—Hardouin, II, 1001.

[11] Cappello, *De Sacramentis,* III, n. 890.

[12] Wernz-Vidal, *Jus Canonicum,* V, n. 686.

[13] C. 1—6, X, *qui matrimonium accusare possunt, vel contra illud testificari,* IV, 18.

[14] C. 5, X, *de testibus et attestationibus,* II, 20.

[15] Feije, *De Impedimentis et Dispensationibus Matrimonialibus,* n. 587.

[16] Hostiensis, *Summa Aurea, De Collusione detegenda* (Lyons, 1586), V, 381.

Indeed in such cases they did not seem to have any great fear of collusion.

The difficulty that preoccupied these writers was to be found in the case in which both spouses claimed that their marriage was invalid. This type of case gave great concern to the commentators of this period.

Esmein declares that this type of case was one of the considerations that prompted the famous Hostiensis to suggest that such cases be publicly denounced, with a call to the relatives of the persons involved or in their default, to a stranger to defend the marriage.[17]

The danger to a valid marriage arising from insufficient defense of validity seems to have been the important consideration in the mind of the writer. Abuses arising from ignorance or malfeasance on the part of judge and curia did not seem to have been a source of worry. This was indeed especially true during the times of the Glossators, and from their silence in this regard it may safely be presumed that the judges of the period were for the most part honest, conscientious and in the main sufficiently learned to fulfill their duties efficiently.[18]

Consequently the law of this period reflects the opinion that the necessity of proof was sufficient to protect the validity of a marriage if contested in court.

Article II

Possible Remote Origins of the Office

I. *A Suggestion of Hostiensis*

While it would be impossible to deny that the office of *Defensor Vinculi* was created by Benedict XIV in the eighteenth century, yet one is tempted to look to a much earlier date in seeking for the more remote origins of the office.

[17] Esmein, *Le Mariage in Droit Canonique*, I, 468; Hostiensis, *Summa Aurea*, IV, *Libellus Accusationis*, 322.

[18] *Encyclopédie Théologique*, article, "Officialité"; *Dictionaire de Droit Canonique*, II, 681.

Pope Benedict XIV has indeed a double claim to distinction. He was not only Pope, but one of the most distinguished canonists of the eighteenth century in his own right.[19] Therefore it may safely be assumed that this Pontiff was well acquainted with the canonical literature of the time, and it is quite possible that some of the suggestions found in older canonical treatises may have found their way into the Benedictine legislation.

Some authors accordingly support the opinion that the germinal idea of the *Defensor Vinculi* is to be found in the writings of Henry of Segusio, the celebrated Hostiensis, who died in 1271.[20]

The text in which Hostiensis seems to suggest a procedure somewhat akin to that now followed by the *Defensor Vinculi* is as follows:

> . . . si quis affinis vel cognitus velit defendere matrimonium, audietur, et demum his deficientibus, quilibet extraneus admittetur. . . . Si ergo aliquis apparet defensor audietur . . .[21]

If the exact interpretation given to this text by Pope Benedict XIV and his contemporaries could be ascertained, it might be possible to estimate its possible influence on the mind of the Pontiff.

Two authors, contemporaries of Benedict XIV, who sufficiently studied the problem to suggest the use of the Promotor *Fiscalis*, make no mention of Hostiensis in this connection. The one, De Justis, in his argumentation appeals to the fact that other writers such as Sanchez, Pontus, Coninck and Laymann declare, *"dissolutio matrimonii est res gravissima,"* while the other, Sperelli merely appeals to practice.[22]

Considering the quotation of Hostiensis alone, it is possible to see in it an idea easy of development into the office of *Defensor*

[19] Albers, P., *Enchiridion Historiae Ecclesiasticae,* III, p. 175.

[20] *"C'est Hostiensis en reálité qui sur l'a inventé"*—Peries, *Procedure Matrimoniale,* 7; Esmein, *Le Mariage en Droit Canonique,* II, 292: *Catholic Encyclopedia,* article, "Hostiensis."

[21] Hostiensis, *Summa Aurea,* lib. iv, *Libellus Accusationis* (*Rub.*), p. 322.

[22] De Justis, *De Dispen. Matrim.* (Lucae, 1726), lib. ii, cap. xvii, nn. 23, 24; Sperelli, *Decisiones Fori Ecclesiastici* (Venice, 1666), *Decis.* 141, n. 68.

Vinculi. Placed in its context, the text loses much of its apparent connection with the *Defensor Vinculi.*

The section of the *Summa Aurea* in which the text appears bears the title "*Libellus Accusationis.*" According to the teaching of the text, anyone, even a stranger, could ask that a marriage vitiated by perpetual diriment impediment be declared null.

The question actually under discussion in this section of the *Summa Aurea* concerns the right of the court to proceed against an absent party. Hostiensis gives as his opinion that, where the absence is due to contempt, the citations are to be issued to insure the validity of the proceedings, and furthermore he adds if the parties legitimately concerned do not wish to make a defense, "*Puto quod accusatio publicanda sit in ecclesia et si affinis vel cognatus velit defendere . . . audietur . . .*" However even in the case where no volunteer defendant (*defensor*) appears, the judge may proceed to the sentence of nullity, provided however, "*Semper citandi sunt quos res tangit et publicandum est an aliquis velit accusare vel defendere.*"

He seems to argue that if anyone can ask that a marriage be declared null, why should not anyone stand in its defense? He is not concerned with an *ex officio* defense of the marriage bond, but solely with the juridical necessity of having someone on the side of the defense.

The "*defensor*" of Hostiensis is nothing more than a witness for the defense, or substitute defendant. In the section of the *Summa Aurea* in which the text under consideration appears, the following may be read:

> Cum agitur de foedere matrimonii, reo absente contumaciter, possunt super impedimento matrimonii recipi testes, dummodo sint legitimi, et ad dicta eorum fertur sententia.[23]

From this text it would seem that the judge could proceed to the pronouncement of the sentence on the information of the *accusator matrimonii.* This tended to make the trial rather one sided, and conducive to error, thus rendering the decision of the judge rather difficult.

[23] X, *Libellus Accusationis,* IV, 18.

Hostiensis did not wish anyone at all to come forth as the *extraneus defensor*. He really wished someone to appear as a witness who had information pertinent to the case. It was for this reason that he suggested that these actions should be denounced in the Church somewhat after the fashion of the pronouncement of the Banns of Marriage. In this manner the case would be brought to the attention of the people, in order that those possessing information would have the opportunity to bring this knowledge to the notice of the court. In short Hostiensis suggested a method of finding witnesses for the side of the absent party, in order that the defendant's side of the case might have some support.

The Glosses to Chapter I, X, Title xviii state:

> In causa matrimoniali, lite non contestata, recipiuntur testes altera parte absente. Ergo altera parte absente at non per contumaceam testes recipiuntur lite non contestata.

Hostiensis seems to be commenting on these Glosses. He is advocating that witnesses should be heard not only on the side of the *accusator*, but also on the other side, even when the *pars conventa* fails to appear. Indirectly of course this offers a certain degree of defense of the marriage, but it is in no way similar to the duties of the *Defensor Vinculi* called into existence by Benedict XIV.

No argument can be drawn from the fact that Hostiensis uses the term "*defensor*" even when coupled with the word *matrimonii*, for the expressions "*matrimonium accusare*," "*matrimonium defendere*" and related expressions were in common use with the canonists of the time. They refer merely to the actions of the *actor* and the *pars conventa* in a matrimonial trial. This usage is merely the normal legal usage of the time. The eighteenth title of the fourth book of the Decretals of Gregory IX, bears the title "*Qui matrimonium accusare possunt, vel contra illud Testificari.*"

Nor was the title *defensor* new in the law, the title itself goes all the way back to Roman Law where the *defensor civitatis* and the *defensor Caesaris* may be found.[24]

It is quite clear that the *defensor* meant by these references is

[24] D. III, *de procuratoribus et defensoribus;* D. I, 19, *de officio procuratoris Caesaris;* Cod. XI, 72, *de procuratoribus.*

one that acts after the fashion of a procurator or an advocate, rather than for the protection of a sacrament as does the *Defensor Vinculi.*

Durandus defines a *defensor* in the following words:

> . . . is qui sine mandato praestita cautione de iudicato solvendo, alium in iudicio defendit . . .

Durandus also discusses whether this *defensor* shall be admitted in matrimonial cases.[25]

It is interesting to note that Durandus who died about 1296, was a contemporary of Hostiensis. Yet in the text cited Durandus seems to use the word "*defensor*" in a sense slightly different from that in which Hostiensis uses it. By "*defensor,*" Durandus means a kind of advocate or lawyer, not a witness, as is evidently the essential meaning of the word in the text of Hostiensis.

The word "*defensor,*" therefore, has a rather wide meaning, and it is impossible to draw any real argument from the mere fact of its use in connection with a person who stands on the side of validity in a marriage case.

Both of these writers refer to someone who upheld the validity of the marriage theoretically on the behalf of one of the parties. The *Defensor Vinculi Matrimonialis* on the contrary does not act on the behalf of either party, he acts simply and solely on the behalf of the validity of the marriage, and herein lies the essential characteristic of the duties of the *Defensor Vinculi.*

II. *Possible Origin in Duties formerly attached to the Office of the Promotor of Justice.*

Cardinal Lega is of the opinion that the office of *Defensor Vinculi* is the result of nothing more than a division of the work formerly given to the Promotor of Justice. He plainly states that the *Defensor Vinculi* is merely a special kind of Promotor of Justice.[26]

In this contention he is supported by the opinions of two prominent

[25] Durandus, I, *Speculum Juris,* lib. I, Pars. III, *de defensore.*

[26] " . . . (qui est species Procuratoris Fiscalis), . . . "—Lega, *Praelectiones de Iudiciis Ecclesiasticis,* I, n. 137.

canonists who wrote before the time of Benedict XIV. These, Sperelli and De Justis by name, both maintain that the *Promotor Fiscalis* should be present to defend the sacramental rights in certain Matrimonial Cases.

Sperelli writes:

> Quod uterque consentiat dissolutioni matrimonii, citandus est Fiscus curiae Episcopus, qui stare debet pro matrimonio ad collusiones et fraudas evitandas . . .[27]

De Justis expresses the same opinion in the following words:

> . . . propterea in casu quo coniuges concorditer pro dissolutione matrimonii stent, debet citari Promotor Fiscalis curiae Episcopalis . . .[28]

Both writers demanded the presence of the *Fiscus* only when both parties claimed the marriage to be invalid, but the importance of their teaching lies in the fact that they demanded an officer of the curia to stand in defense of the marriage for the avoidance of collusion and fraud. This duty certainly shows a basic similarity to that of the *Defensor Vinculi.*

This was more than a practice suggested by these writers, it was the actual method of procedure followed in many courts.

In an appeal submitted to the Sacred Congregation of the Council on September 30, 1719, the assertion is found that the interrogations were made by the *Fiscus*. The case concerned was a matrimonial one in which the claim was made that the marriage was null.[29]

This case does not stand alone; there are several others to be found in the collection of summaries and opinions made by Benedict XIV. This was a collection of selected decisions of the Sacred Congregation of the Council, edited by Prosper Lambertini, the then Secretary of the Congregation who later became Pope Benedict XIV.

Another of these summaries states that a certain curia decided to send a marriage case directly to the Sacred Congregation for trial,

[27] *Decisiones Fori Ecclesiastici,* Vol. II, *Decisio,* 141, n. 68.

[28] *De Dispensationibus Matrim.* (Lucae, 1726), lib. II, cap. xvii, n. 24.

[29] Benedict XIV, *Quaestiones Canonicae et Morales* (Prati, 1844), I, *Quaest.* CXX, p. 137.

because the office of the *Promotor Fiscalis* was unfilled at the time.[80]

Still another case gives a clearer picture of the *Fiscus* performing duties that now pertain to the *Defensor Vinculi*.

The summary reads in part as follows:

> . . . citato patre Catharinae, et eodem negligente iure prosequi suae filiae, quae est absens, et ignoratur, in quo loco degat, danda esse a Fiscali curiae interrogatoria ex officio.[81]

These few citations show clearly that the practice of citing the Promotor of Justice (then known as the *Fiscus*) to take up the defense of undefended marriage cases was sufficiently common to permit reference to the practice without explanatory comment.

The manner in which these cases are described shows that the practice was not regarded as extraordinary, but rather was considered to be the usual method of procedure when there was no one to defend the validity of a contested marriage before the court.

Regardless of how widespread the practice was, it was sufficiently developed to present a germinal idea which was quite capable of development into the office of *Defensor Vinculi.* That Benedict XIV was well acquainted with the practice is proven by the fact that he edited the cases to which reference has just been made. The practice certainly does lend support to the view that the *Defensor Vinculi* represents a division of the work originally given to the *Procurator Fiscalis*.

In this connection it is also important to bear in mind that the duties of the *Procurator Fiscalis* were not well defined at the time of Benedict XIV.[82] The office as yet was not one of common law, and hence its rights and their extent were somewhat nebulous. In criminal procedure the duties of the *Fiscus* were sufficiently defined to cause Pellegrini to state that the presence of the *Fiscus* was required under pain of nullity,[83] but the same cannot be said with regard to his duties in other forms of procedure.

[80] *Op. cit., Quaest.*, CCXXVI, p. 295.

[81] *Op. cit., Quaest.*, CCCLVI, p. 463.

[82] Lega, *Praelectiones,* I, n. 139.

[83] *Praxis Vicariorum* (Venice, 1706), Part IV, Sect. I, n. 20.

Outside of those places where this practice was in vogue, it would seem that the law was satisfied that the necessity of providing proof for the nullity of a marriage was sufficient to protect the sacrament if it were in reality valid. This seems to have been the general attitude of the law up until the introduction of the new laws of Benedict XIV.

The cases submitted to the Sacred Congregation of the Council, to which reference has been made, show that in certain localities, the *Fiscus* was called in to defend the validity of the sacrament of Marriage when neither of the married parties would do so. This was only natural. A trial is essentially a conflict, but a conflict is rather difficult when there is no opposition. The *Fiscus* was called in to supply the necessary opposition, and he did so by upholding the validity of the marriage before the court.

This use of the *Fiscus* is in complete agreement with the teaching of both Sperelli and De Justis. They base their practice on two grounds. On the one hand they appeal to the fact that marriage was commonly regarded as a *res gravissima* in the law, and on the other hand they appeal to practice. Either of these arguments was sufficient to justify their teaching. To one searching for the origins of the office of *Defensor Vinculi*, the argument based on the fact that marriage is a *res gravissima* is of some interest, especially since Benedict XIV in constituting the office of *Defensor Vinculi* characterizes marriage as *magnum in Ecclesia Sacramentum.*

In fact the need for the office of *Defensor Vinculi* could not be admitted unless marriage was at least *res gravissima.*

The use of the *Fiscus* for the defense of undefended marriages was a practice that is easily understood. The duties of the *Fiscus* were still somewhat undefined and nebulous in the eighteenth century. His duties were described only in very general terms such as the following: ". . . *defendere fiscalia, sunt autem fiscalia, ea in quibus agitur de publica pecunia vel indicta.*"[34] They were therefore elastic and could be extended by the Bishop to the protection of all public rights and laws.

Sperelli and De Justis were not radical innovators therefore,

[34] Pellegrini, *Praxis Vicariorum*, Part IV, Sect. II, n. 69.

when they taught that the *Fiscus* should be called in to defend undefended marriage cases, for, as Lega states: *"Quum agatur de matrimonio ut sacramento, iurium inde fluentium seu actio iudicialis non tantum competat partibus, sed ipsi Reipublicae."* [35]

The office of *Promotor Fiscalis* was formally erected for the Diocese and Province of Rome in the year 1724 by Pope Benedict XIII, an indication that the office was generally adopted throughout the Church by that time.[36]

It is also worthy of note that it was only shortly before in the year 1708, that Clement XI instituted the office of *Promotor Fidei,* a type of *Promotor Fiscalis,* for the prevention and detection of fraud in the canonization process.[37] The revealing fact is that the *Defensor Vinculi* has the same function in the matrimonial trial as the *Promotor Fidei* in the canonization process. In addition to the striking resemblance in the general purpose of the two offices, the likeness is heightened by the requirement that both officials have to be present at all sessions under pain of nullifying the *acta,* and that both have the right to examine the *acta* at any time during the progress of the respective processes.

These facts are rendered all the more revealing when it is recalled that Pope Benedict XIV held the office of *Promotor Fidei* for twenty years before he became Pope.[38] As a consequence one is forced to conclude that in all probability the *Defensor Vinculi* is nothing more than a *Promotor Fidei* adapted to the matrimonial trial, which brings to mind the fact that the *Promotor Fidei* is merely a specialized *Promotor Fiscalis.*

With these facts in mind the development that gave rise to the *Defensor Vinculi* is rather evident, and the argument that they supply should not be minimized. The long incumbency of Benedict XIV in the office of *Promotor Fidei,* as well as the resemblances between

[35] *Praelectiones,* IV, n. 414.

[36] Benedict XIV, *De Synodo Dioecesana* (Rome, 1748), lib. IV, cap. iii, n. 8.

[37] Benedict XIV, *De Serv. Dei Beat. et Beatorum Canoniz.,* T. I., lib. X, cap. xviii, *pars* 5 and 10.

[38] *Catholic Encyclopedia,* articles, *"Promoter Fidei"* and *"Benedict XIV."*

this office and that of *Defensor Vinculi* serve to forge a rather strong bond between the two offices.

Benedict himself gives added force to this view, when in writing on the canonization process, he clearly states that, because of the special nature of the work demanded of the *Promotor Fidei,* and because of the fact that the *Fiscus* was often a layman, the two offices should be conferred on different persons.[39]

In the light of these facts, it is easy to conceive that the Pope, having seen the success of the office of *Promotor Fidei* which evolved from the *Fiscus,* decided to extend the evolution a step further, giving us the *Defensor Vinculi,* who was then the product of a development in a direct line from the *Promotor Fiscalis.*

In conclusion it must be admitted that the opinion is at least truly probable which derives the office of *Defensor Vinculi* from that of the Promotor of Justice (the *Fiscus*). As for the other opinion, there is little real evidence to indicate that the ideas of Hostiensis had any connection with the conception of the *Defensor Vinculi* in the mind of Pope Benedict XIV.

Article III

The Conditions That Impelled the Pope to Institute the Office of *Defensor Vinculi*

By the time the eighteenth century was approaching the half way mark, the evils and abuses that afflicted the dispensation of justice in matrimonial trials had become sufficiently pronounced to demand immediate and decisive attention. Collusion and fraud arising from the machinations of the married parties seeking release, were no longer the only causes at the seat of the trouble, but frequently the very judges who dispensed justice in the name of the Church were not above suspicion. It came to be realized that some of these judges not only lacked the necessary knowledge, but were not even above reproach both in their honesty and in the integrity of

[39] *De Serv. Dei Beat. et Beatorum Canoniz.,* T. I, lib. I, *cap.* xviii, *pars* 5 and 10.

their Faith.[40] It was because of the judicial acts of judges of this type that Benedict had to include among his complaints, "*iudicum ignorantiam et malitiam.*" [41]

That these conditions were somewhat general is evidenced by the Encyclical Letter "*Quamvis Paternae,*" [42] addressed to the whole Church. Poland, however, seems to have been a special offender in this manner for the Pope saw fit under the date of April 11, 1741, to despatch to this country a special letter of admonition. In the letter the Pope deplores the great scandal that had arisen because of the laxity of their courts whereby certain individuals were enabled to contract three and four successive marriages while their former consorts were still living.[43]

Neither this letter, nor the subsequent laws contained in the constitution "*Dei Miseratione*" [44] were sufficient to remedy these evils, for the Pope found necessary to despatch another encyclical to Poland in the year 1743, in which he threatened that, if conditions did not improve, would reserve all matrimonial cases in Poland to the Holy See, even in first instance.[45]

Conditions such as these do not arise over night. The causes of so widespread a condition are seldom simple or traceable to a single factor. The Europe of the seventeenth century was most restless, the spirit of controversy permeated everywhere.

The indissolubility of marriage was defined by the Council of Trent, and the opposition to the definition was not slow in showing itself. The fact that the Schismatic Orthodox Church granted absolute divorce for adultery supplied the fuel to feed the fire. Attempts were made to show that the canon of the Council of Trent [46] was merely disciplinary and not doctrinal.

[40] Benedict XIV, const., *Quamvis Paternae,* August 26, 1741—*Fontes,* n. 315.

[41] *Ibid.*

[42] Benedict XIV, August 26, 1741—*Fontes,* n. 315.

[43] Benedict XIV, Litt., encycl., *Matrimonii,* April 11, 1741—*Fontes, n.* 307.

[44] *Fontes,* n. 318.

[45] Benedict XIV, Litt, encycl., *Nimiam Licentiam,* May 18, 1743—*Fontes,* n. 337.

[46] *Conc. Trid.,* Sess. XXIV, *De Sacramento Matrimonii,* c. 7; Joyce, *Christian Marriage,* p. 395.

The Catholics could hardly escape being influenced by this practice indulged in by their Protestant and schismatic neighbors, and consequently their own attitude to the sacrament was at times far from orthodox.

All in all, the abuses in connection with the administration of the Church courts in the eighteenth century were by no means phenomena without cause, as even this cursory consideration indicates.

The demoralizing spirit made itself felt within the Church itself, creating a condition that called for prompt and effective remedial action.

The decrees of the Council of Trent served to keep these forces in check, but they were unable to thwart completely the newly arisen evils.[47] It remained for Benedict XIV to devise the specific remedy, a set of laws that because of their serviceability have remained unchanged down to this day, now being embodied in the Code of Canon Law.[48]

So it was that Benedict XIV brought to a successful culmination a long series of efforts to develop and protect the administration of justice in the courts of the Church especially where the sacrament of Marriage was concerned.[49]

[47] *Conc. Trid.*, Sess. XXV, *de reform.*, cap. 10, Sess. XXIV, *de reform.*, cap. 20.

[48] Benedict XIV, const., *Dei Miseratione,* November 3, 1741—*Fontes,* n. 38.

[49] C. T, *de iudiciis,* II, 1, in Clem.; *Conc. Trid.*, Sess. XXIV, *de reform.*, cap. 20, Sess. XXV, *de reform.*, cap. 10; c. 7, Harduinus, *Acta Conc.*, VII, 1083, VII, 1817.

CHAPTER II

SOME GENERAL NOTIONS IN CONNECTION WITH THE OFFICE OF *DEFENSOR VINCULI*

ARTICLE I

THE APPOINTMENT OF THE *Defensor Vinculi*

THE appointment of the *Defensor Vinculi* according to the words of canon 1589 [1] belongs to the Ordinary. The term "local ordinary" in the eyes of the Code of Canon Law includes all residential Bishops, Abbots nullius, Prelates nullius and their Vicars General; also Administrators Apostolic, and Vicars or Prefects Apostolic, as well as all those who succeed to their powers according to the provisions of the law.[2]

These officials are all regarded as local ordinaries (*ordinarii locorum*) by the law.[3] The Code, however, does not include under the term "local ordinary" major religious superiors of clerical exempt congregations or Orders. These may be local ordinaries only in the event that they are also Abbots or Prelates *nullius*.

What then is the meaning of the words *"Ordinarii est . . ."* in canon 1589? All residential Bishops, Abbots or Prelates nullius, Vicars, Administrators, or Prefects Apostolic certainly can elect the *Defensor Vinculi* for their own territory.

The residential Bishops, Abbots *nullius* and Prelates *nullius* are empowered to elect a Vicar General for their territories. The other ordinaries cannot do so; they can, it is true, appoint a pro-vicar, a pro-prefect or a Vicar Delegate, but these officials are not ordinaries, nor do they enjoy the plenitude of power that the Vicar General does. *Sede vacante* or *sede impedita* certain of these quasi-vicars

1 "Ordinarii est . . . vinculi defensorem eligere. . . . "

2 Canon 198, § 1.

3 Canon 198, § 2.

general succeed to the power of their ordinaries, and only then do they become ordinaries within the meaning of the law.[4]

Vicars and Prefects Apostolic are empowered to appoint a Vicar Delegate,[5] an official to whom is conceded practically all the spiritual and temporal jurisdiction that the Code is wont to grant to the Vicar General.[6]

This does not, however, give to the Vicar Delegate a right to appoint a *Defensor Vinculi* without special mandate from the Bishop. The right of the Vicar General to appoint the *Defensor Vinculi* derives from the fact that he is an ordinary in the sense of canon 198, and is in no way limited in the Law in the exercise of his power in connection with the appointment of the *Defensor Vinculi.*

The Vicar Delegate while very similar to a Vicar General, is nevertheless essentially different. He does not constitute one person with the Vicar or Prefect Apostolic in the eyes of the law, and does not lose his power with the cessation of the jurisdiction of the Vicar or Prefect Apostolic.[7]

It is essentially the unity of person of the Vicar General with the bishop that constitutes him an Ordinary in the legal sense of the word. This condition is not verified in the case of the Vicar Delegate, who certainly cannot be an Ordinary within the meaning of the law [8] since he does not even enjoy the exercise of ordinary power, possessing only the delegated power of the Prefect or Vicar Apostolic.[9]

Not being an Ordinary, he is certainly not empowered by canon 1589, §1, to appoint a *Defensor Vinculi.*

According to a strict interpretation of the canons it would seem that the Vicar General can appoint the *Defensor Vinculi.* Nor does he seem to need a special mandate, for he is an Ordinary in the sense

[4] Canons 429, § 1; 198; § 1; Chelodi, *Jus de Personis,* p. 300; Wernz-Vidal, *Jus Canonicum,* III, n. 636; Wernz-Vidal, *Jus Canonicum,* III, n. 545.

[5] *AAS,* XII (1920), 120.

[6] Vermeersch-Creusen, *Epitome,* I, n. 366, 2; "Vermeersch" in *Periodica,* IX (1921), 24.

[7] Vermeersch-Creusen, *Epitome,* I, n. 366, 2.

[8] Canon 198.

[9] *Jus Pontificium,* III (1923), 145.

of the law, and is not expressly excluded by canon 1589,[10] or any other canon of the Code.

This opinion seems to be quite certain, at least its examination in the light of the Code fails to disclose any defect in it.

True it has received little mention by commentators, but then only a few authors have studied the law of the *Defensor Vinculi* with any degree of thoroughness. An author explaining the whole of the Fourth Book cannot be expected to go into all details of the law.

In the commentary of Wernz-Vidal, the statement is made that it seems the *Defensor Vinculi* may be appointed by the Vicar General or the *Officialis,* only when these latter officials were possessed of the special mandate of the bishop.[11]

It is well to bear in mind that while the *Officialis* possesses ordinary power [12] yet he is not an Ordinary in the legal sense of the word as explained in canon 198, and therefore he is not the *"ordinarius"* of canon 1589, and cannot consequently appoint the *Defensor Vinculi* without special mandate.

In addition, it is likewise well to consider, that while the *Officialis* is indeed the Bishop's other self in judicial matters, as the Vicar General is in administrative matters, nevertheless the act of appointing a *Defensor Vinculi* is an administrative rather than a judicial act.

There is but one case where the judge may appoint the *Defensor Vinculi.* It is the case of a judge delegated specially by the Holy See. Under these circumstances this judge would be free to use the ministers of the diocesan curia, or select others himself, unless his rescript of delegation limited his power in this respect. This would occur only in an exceptional case at present, as such cases would be regulated in this matter by the judge's rescript of delegation.

The question of the right of the *Officialis* to appoint the *Defensor Vinculi* by virtue of special mandate does not enter into the question in any way. The power of the Bishop is ordinary, and he is perfectly free to delegate either in whole or in part.[13]

[10] Canon 198, § 1, " . . . eorumque Vicarius Generalis, . . . "; canon 1589.

[11] Wernz-Vidal, *Jus Canonicum,* VI, n. 114.

[12] Canon 1573, §1: ". . . cum potestate ordinaria iudicandi . . ."

[13] Canons 198, § 1; 199, §1.

Vidal bases his restriction of the power of the Vicar General in this instance on the doctrine of Benedict XIV, in the *De Synodo Dioecesana,* II, 8, n. 2, where the restricting clause reads: ". . . *quae sunt merae liberalitatis et gratiae, vel speciem habet alienationis* . . ." and therefore concludes that the Vicar General would need a special mandate, for the free conferring of an office or benefice. Indeed the designation of the Promotor of Justice or the *Defensor Vinculi* is an act of free nomination to an important diocesan office.

But where does this restriction derive from in the Code? Certainly not from the necessity of a mandate imposed on the Vicar General by canon 152,[14] for this canon touches ecclesiastical offices in the strict sense only. Canon 145 tells us that "*in iure*" ecclesiastical office is always to be understood in the *strict sense,* unless the context shows otherwise. This phrase "*in iure*" applies not only to the Code, but to all existing law.

The first part of the same canon defines ecclesiastical office in the *strict sense,* and lays down certain requirements. The canon requires that the office must participate in some way in ecclesiastical power either of orders or jurisdiction. The office of *Defensor Vinculi* has attached to it many rights, but none of them demands the exercise of power or jurisdiction.[15] The *Defensor Vinculi* is essentially nothing more than a privileged party to the Matrimonial trial whose duty it is to protect the sanctity of the sacrament of Marriage, by preventing it from being unwarrantably declared null. Nor may one use the fact that the *Defensor Vinculi* is enumerated among the officials of the Diocesan Curia in canon 363 § 2, in order to weaken the contention that the office is not an office in the *strict sense.* The canon immediately following is a confession that some of these offices are not offices in the *strict sense.* If these offices were all offices in the *strict sense,* there would be no necessity for the provision of canon 364, §1, since they would all fall under the requirement of

[14] "Loci ordinarius ius habet providendi officiis ecclesiasticis in proprio territorio, nisi aliud probetur; hac tamen potestate caret Vicarius Generalis sine mandato speciali"; *cf.* also Campagna, *Il Vicario Generale,* p. 128.

[15] A Coronata, *De Processibus,* p. 36, m. 1124; Roberti, *De Processibus,* I, p. 194.

canon 159, which demands the provision of all offices to be made in writing.

Therefore the restriction of canon 152 has no effect on the right of the Vicar General to appoint the *Defensor Vinculi,* since the canon applies only to the appointment to offices that are such in the strict sense.

The *Defensor Vinculi* is a member of the Diocesan Curia, the members of which body according to canon 363, §1, either rule the diocese in the name of the bishop, or help him in its general administration. These officials are personally attached to the bishop, they are the members of his private cabinet, and hence they should be personally appointed by the Bishop. In normal circumstances, therefore, it would be wrong for the Vicar General to appoint the *Defensor Vinculi* without being instructed by the Bishop, both because of the intimate connection of the *Defensor* with the Curia of the Bishop, and also because he is bound to act in accordance with the mind and will of the Bishop.[16] This is an important post in the diocese and in practice the Bishop certainly is to be presumed to wish to fill it himself.

Most authors in their general treatment of the Curia simply state that the members are to be appointed by the Bishop, and that the appointment must be in writing.[17] This they do without giving any apparent thought to the special canon covering the appointment of the *Defensor Vinculi* and the Promotor of Justice. Then too, they are non-committal in their direct reference to the appointment of the *Defensor Vinculi* and the Promotor of Justice.

The importance of the office too, seems to imply that the Bishop should fill the position personally, at least by selecting the regular incumbent, and the Code does intend the office to be filled by a permanent appointee in a settled diocese. Considering these circumstances it would at least be imprudent for the Vicar General to make this appointment without special instructions from the Bishop, because he would seem to be acting in opposition to canon 369, § 2.

It seems certain, therefore, that the Vicar General may validly

[16] Canon 369, § 2.

[17] Chelodi, *Jus de Personis,* p. 327; Wernz-Vidal, *Jus Canonicum,* II, p. 675; Vermeersch-Creusen, *Epitome,* I, p. 282, n. 432, 2; III, p. 20, n. 43, 3.

and licitly appoint the *Defensor Vinculi* at least for one or for several cases when the Bishop cannot be reached.

This necessity might arise even in a well-run and well-organized diocese, in the case where an exception of suspicion has been accepted against the regular *Defensor Vinculi*, thus preventing him from acting in the case, an occurrence which might easily occur when the Bishop was away.[18] In this case there can be advanced no certain argument against the validity or the liceity of the appointment made by the Vicar General. He certainly acts validly for he is empowered by canons 1589 and 198, §1. He is the ordinary in the sense of the Code, and he is consequently empowered to act.

While it is true that few authors refer to this fact, it seems that many are merely silent rather than in disagreement. For the most part they are covering broad fields, and cannot offer to special phases too much consideration or space.[19]

The *Defensor Vinculi* may be appointed by the Vicar Capitular though he cannot be removed by him, since the Vicar Capitular is restricted in this regard by the Code itself.[20]

[20] Canon 1590, § 1.

If the office of the *Defensor Vinculi* were to become vacant during the period that the diocese is under the rule of the *Vicar Capitular*, it might become necessary for the *Vicar Capitular* to appoint a *Defensor Vinculi*. The *Vicar Capitular* is an Ordinary in the meaning of the Code of Canon Law.[21] He is therefore empowered by the terms of canon 1589, §1 to appoint the *Defensor Vinculi*. For a confirmation of this conclusion reference may be made to the almost parallel case indicated in canon 1573, § 7. In this case the *Officialis* is elected Vicar Capitular, the office of *Officialis* becomes vacant and it is the duty of the *Vicar Capitular* to name the new *Officialis*.

This is exactly what would happen if the office of *Defensor Vinculi* were to become vacant during the rule of the Vicar Capitular, who

[18] *Cf.* canon 1613, §§ 1, 2.

[19] Roberti, *De Processibus*, I, 198; Wernz-Vidal, *Jus Canonicum*, VI, 101; Vermeersch-Creusen, III, p. 20; Payen, *De Matrimonio*, III, n. 2661; A Coronata, *De Processibus*, p. 37, n. 1124, 2°. *Noval, De Processibus*, n. 147.

[21] Canon 198, § 1: ". . . itemque ii qui praedictis deficientibus interim ex iuris praescripto aut ex probatis constitutionibus succedunt in regimine; . . ."

is the Ordinary and has all the powers of the Ordinary, except in those things in which he is restricted by law.

Not only is the power to appoint the *Defensor Vinculi* vested in the Vicar Capitular as the Ordinary, but he also has an obligation to appoint one. This is clearly implied by the words of the canon ". . . *Constituatur in dioecesi promotor justitiae et defensor vinculi.* . . ."[22] This clearly indicates that it is the intention of the Holy See to have a permanently appointed *Defensor Vinculi* in every fully organized diocese.

The wording of all the important forms of the Pre-Code Law also tends to confirm the fact that it is the will of the lawgiver to have a permanently appointed *Defensor Vinculi* in every properly organized diocese.[23]

This was the rule even before the Code, as is witnessed by Cardinal Gasparri's reference to the contrary practice as an exception.

The Nomination of the *Defensor Vinculi* must be in writing.[24] The reason for this law is obvious, for the appointment is given in this form in order that it will lend itself to easy and incontrovertible proof. This is especially necessary inasmuch as the validity or the nullity of the trial may depend on the assistance or a validly appointed *Defensor Vinculi.*

While the *Defensor Vinculi* owes his appointment to the Ordinary, yet when he acts before the court he is subject to the judge and owes him reverence and obedience.[25]

The judge is empowered to punish all those who do not render to him and the court due reverence and obedience. A person may offend the court directly when he shows contempt to the judge himself, or indirectly when the offense is either directed at those present, or is given by deliberate disobedience of the discipline that governs the trial.[26]

[22] Canon 1586.

[23] Benedict XIV, *"Dei Miseratione,"* November 3, 1741, n. 5—*Fontes,* n. 318; S. C. S. Officii, Instr. (*ad Ep. Rituum Orient.*), a. 1883, n. 7—*Fontes,* n. 1076; S. C. C., Instr., August 22, 1840—*Fontes,* n. 4069, p. 346; Gasparri, II (1891), n. 1174 (1); Augustine, *Commentary,* V, p. 412; Sipos, *Enchiridion,* 812.

[24] Canon 364, § 1; Payen, *De Matrimonio,* III, n. 2661.

[25] Canon 1640, § 2; Wernz-Vidal, *Jus Canonicum,* VI, n. 199.

[26] Noval, *De Processibus,* I, 148.

The *Defensor,* one of the officials of the Curia, is also liable to punishment by the judge for failure to perform his duties and for culpable neglect in performance thereof.[27]

Since the *Defensor* is one of the officials of the Curia, the judge is empowered directly by the Code to punish him for infractions of this nature, and even to remove him if such action is warranted.[28]

It may seem somewhat contradictory at first sight that the judge can even remove these officials, the appointment of whom must be made by the Bishop. The Bishop of course can punish them, if the judge wishes to refer the matter to him.[29] But it must be remembered that when the judge, the *Officialis,* punishes a negligent member of the Curia he is the Bishop's other self in judicial matters, and that essentially he is using and sharing the Bishop's judicial power, for the Bishop always has the right to try a case himself in place of the ecclesiastic he has empowered with his judicial jurisdiction.[30]

The Code itself too, in another section expressly imposes on the judge the obligation to force the *Defensor* to perform his duties if he is remiss or negligent in their fulfillment. This means that the judge has the power to enforce action on the part of the negligent *Defensor* with threats of punishment. The Code certainly does not wish the judge to make empty threats, so this duty implies that the judge has the power actually to impose these punishments.[31]

The judge not only has the right and the duty to impose penalties strictly speaking, but also the power and the duty to condemn a negligent *Defensor* to make good pecuniary or other loss that he has occasioned.[32]

The punishments that the judge can impose for these infractions

[27] Canon 1625, § 3; Noval, *De Processibus,* I, 131.

[28] Canon 1625, § 1, " . . . non exclusa officii privatione"; Canon 1625, § 3, "Eisdem sanctionibus subsunt tribunali officiales et adiutores, si officio suo, ut supra, defuerint, quos omnes etiam iudex punire potest"; Wernz-Vidal, *Jus Canonicum,* VI, 135.

[29] Canon 1625, § 1; Canon 1625, § 3.

[30] Canons 1572, § 1, 1578.

[31] Canon 1986; Noval, *De Processibus,* I, 578; De Becker, *De Matrimonio* (Edit. 1931), p. 278.

[32] Canon 1625, § 1, " . . . tenentur de damnis . . . "; Noval, *De Processibus,* I, 131.

of course must be proportionate to the gravity of the offense. The offender too, is responsible for loss ensuing from an act gravely culpable on his part, or working grave injustice on the parties or others involved in the case.

Since this is a matter that is concerned with justice, the punishments and the damages may be inflicted not only at the instance of the injured party or parties, but also *ex officio*.[33]

Article II

The Tenure of Office of the *Defensor Vinculi*

The Bishop may appoint a *Defensor Vinculi* for all cases in which his presence is required or only for an individual case as often as the need arises.[34]

The necessity for the appointing of a special *Defensor Vinculi* may arise even in a diocese which has a regular incumbent in this office. This may arise in a variety of ways, the regular *Defensor* may be ill, then again he may be related to one of the parties to the trial, or he may have acted in the same case in some other capacity previously, that would exclude him from acting in the case. The appointment of the special *Defensor Vinculi* naturally lapses with the conclusion of the case for which he was appointed.

However if the *Defensor* was appointed for all cases then his appointment may be terminated by removal by the bishop, resignation, and of course through his own incapacitation.

The Bishop may remove him for just cause.[35] This means that the Bishop or the Ordinary should have some reason for the removal more than mere displeasure. The Bishop, however, can validly remove him without reason, but such action would be illicit, as it is contrary to the Code. In the removal the Bishop can, of course, proceed without canonical process.

The *Officialis*, as has been pointed out, may remove him in connection with the maintenance of the discipline of the court.[36]

[33] Canon 1625, §1; Wernz-Vidal, *Jus Canonicum*, VI, 135.
[34] Canon 1588, § 2.
[35] Canon 1590, § 2.
[36] *Cf.* Supra; canon 1625.

The Vicar General presents a problem that is not quite as simple of solution. As has already been indicated in this study, the Vicar General is in no way prevented by the law from appointing a *Defensor Vinculi*. But may he remove him? If the removal is a penal act, then the Vicar General cannot remove the *Defensor Vinculi*, because canon 2220, § 2, takes away from him all right to impose penalties without the special mandate of the Bishop. If the Vicar General himself has appointed the *Defensor Vinculi* there seems to be no apparent reason why he cannot remove the *Defensor Vinculi* for administrative reasons, since all the restrictions in the Code apply only to offices in the strict sense.[37] However, here the Vicar General would also be obliged to observe the wishes of the Bishop in the matter, an obligation which is imposed on him by canon 369, § 2.

If the Bishop had appointed the *Defensor Vinculi*, the Vicar General would need at least the informal consent of the Bishop, which might be derived from the general policy indicated in the instructions given to him by the Bishop. Otherwise he could hardly be regarded as acting in conformity with the mind and wishes of the Bishop, in removing a man appointed by him.[38]

The *Defensor Vinculi* may also cease from office by incurring excommunication, which takes away from the delinquent the right to place legitimate acts.[39] Acts placed in disobedience of this prohibition are illicit if placed before condemnatory or declaratory sentence, invalid if placed after it.[40]

Suspension from office would also deprive the *Defensor Vinculi* of the exercise of his duties, since this punishment forbids not only the placing of all acts of power or jurisdiction, but forbids also the mere exercise of the administration of an office.[41]

Acts placed in violation of the suspension would be illicit before condemnatory or declarative sentence, invalid after the pronouncement of such sentence.[42]

[37] Canon 145, § 2.
[38] Canon 369, § 2.
[39] Canon 2263.
[40] Canon 2264.
[41] Canon 2279, § 1.
[42] Canons 2283, 2265; Cocchi, *De Delictis et Poenis*, p. 176.

If the see were to become vacant, through death, transfer or incapacity of the Bishop, the *Defensor Vinculi* continues in office, and cannot be removed by the Vicar Capitular.[43]

He may be removed, however, by an Apostolic Administrator who is permanently appointed. He cannot be removed by the temporarily appointed Administrator, who in all things is to be considered as the Vicar Capitular. The temporary Administrator is merely a substitute for the Vicar Capitular and is under all the restrictions of the latter.[44]

If the Vicar Capitular through the permanent cessation from office of the *Defensor Vinculi,* should find it necessary to appoint one, he, of course, can do so for all cases without any restriction. In doing so, he cannot be regarded as violating the law of canon 436 [45] for he is not making any permanent change in the regime of the diocese for the last phrase of canon 1590, § 1 [46] gives the incoming prelate the right to refuse confirmation to the holder of the office of *Defensor Vinculi* if he so desires.

In the event of vacancy in the office of the *Defensor Vinculi,* the Vicar Capitular may find it almost necessary to appoint a *Defensor* for all cases, because the number of cases might make it extremely inconvenient for him to appoint one for each case.

In the normal routine during the interval between the two Bishops, the *Defensor* will usually keep his office, and continue to function in it. However, with the advent of the new Ordinary he will need confirmation. This will also hold for the *Defensor* appointed with the general mandate by the Vicar Capitular if the latter has been forced to do so.[47]

However this does not mean that with the arrival of the new incumbent in the see, the *Defensor* automatically lapses from office. The *Defensor Vinculi* continues in office until he has received notice of the Bishop's failure to confirm him in his office.[48]

This is in accord with the way that the Church desires jurisdic-

[43] Canon 1590, § 1.

[44] Canons 1590, §§ 1, 2; 315, §§ 1, 2, 1°; Noval, *De Judiciis,* n. 148.

[45] "Sede vacante nihil innovetur."

[46] " . . . adveniente autem novo praelato, indigent confirmatione."

[47] Canon 1590, § 1.

[48] Roberti, *De Processibus,* I, p. 199; Noval, Pars. I, *De Judiciis,* n. 116.

tion, and appointment to important offices to be revoked.[49] According to which practice, the one holding the office or enjoying the jurisdiction, must be informed of his removal and only at this point does the revocation or the removal become effective. While it is doubtful that the *Defensor* may be considered as exercising jurisdiction or power even in a broad sense, and while it is not certain that he holds an office in the strict sense, still his office is an important one from this same aspect. This, because of the fact that his action and presence in the case is required for validity. The same reason exists here, that exists in the case of a judge or a confessor. If this doctrine is not followed in this case, a whole session of a trial might be rendered null, due to the fact that the *Defensor* in the case did not know that his appointment had failed of confirmation.

A glance at canon 20 will also give support to the practice indicated in the preceding paragraphs. The law indeed does not expressly provide for this transaction, but it is certainly similar to that of the withdrawal of an office in the strict sense or jurisdiction. Consequently the refusal of confirmation should be intimated to the holder of the office of *Defensor Vinculi.*

Article III

The Personal Requirements of the *Defensor Vinculi*

The Code lays down certain requirements that ought to be found in one competent to hold the office of *Defensor Vinculi.* In other words it lays down the notes of fitness for the holder of this office.[50] The Code in the first place demands that the *Defensor* be a priest, although this was not originally a requirement for the holder of the office of *Defensor Vinculi.* However, it will be noticed that the law that was in force before the Code preferred the holder of this office to be a priest or at least an ecclesiastic.[51]

[49] Canons 371, 207; 192, § 3, 2°; Ayrinhac, *General Legislation,* p. 367; Vermeersch-Creusen, *Epitome,* I, n. 270; Ojetti, *Comment,* II, p. 138, " . . . privatio tamen effectum non habet, nisi postquam fuerit a Superiore intimata . . . "; Chelodi, *Jus de Personis,* p. 253, n. 149.

[50] Canon 1589, § 1.

[51] Benedict XIV, const. *Dei Miseratione,* November 3, 1741, n. 5—*Fontes,*

The Roman Instructions of the last century, all require an ecclesiastic to be chosen as *Defensor Vinculi*,[52] making it evident that the positive demand of the Code of Canon Law requiring the holder of the office be a priest is not a sudden change in the law.

The constitution *"Dei Miseratione"* demanded in the *Defensor* both knowledge of the law and probity of life.[53] The Code is more explicit in making its requirements, for it demands integrity of reputation, and the possession of the Doctorate in Canon Law, or commensurate knowledge. It also demands that the *Defensor* be a man of proven prudence, and zeal for justice. This means that the person must have a good reputation, but it is sufficient that the good character be merely negative, that is that it has never been impeached.[54] The necessity of a knowledge of Canon Law on the part of the *Defensor Vinculi* is evident when one considers his duties with any degree of thoroughness. The Code demands that he have either the Degree of Doctor of Canon Law or equivalent knowledge. Many *Defensores* have not received this degree but have been engaged in the study and practice of Canon Law and Moral Theology for many years. Hence they are admirably prepared to fill this office, and the Code recognizes their competency. They must also have proven themselves prudent and zealous for justice. The Code here implies that their prudence and zeal must be positively proven and not merely negative.[55]

The common law of the Church also demands that the *Defensor Vinculi* be free from the exception of suspicion in the technical sense of the law. This means that there must be no legal claim against him that would leave him open to the charge of being prejudiced for

n. 318, " . . . si fieri potest ex ecclesiastico coetu . . . "; Gasparri, *De Matrimonio* (1891 edit.), II, n. 1174, nota 3.

[52] Inst. S. C. S. Officii (*ad Ep. Rituum Orient.*), a. 1883, Tit., II, n. 7; (this instruction was sent to the United States of America in the same year)—*Fontes*, n. 1076.

[53] N. 5—*Fontes*, n. 318, ". . . juris scientia, pariter, et vitae probitate praedita . . . "

[54] Noval, I, *De Processibus*, Pars. I, p. 83, n. 147.

[55] Canon 1589, § 1, " . . . ac prudentiae et justitiae zelo probati . . . "; Noval, *De Processibus*, Pars. I, n. 147, p. 83.

or against either party to the trial. In this regard he is bound by the same restrictions as is the judge and his assistant judges.[56]

The reason behind this legislation is, that the Judge, the Promotor of Justice and the *Defensor Vinculi,* are all acting in the behalf of justice and the common good. Hence they should be free from all suspicion of bias to one side or the other.[57]

It is for this reason that the Judge, the Promotor of Justice and the *Defensor Vinculi* are open to the exception of suspicion, and bound to abstain from acting under the following circumstances.[58]

These three officials are bound to withdraw from a case whenever they are related to one of the parties in the case by consanguinity or affinity in any degree of the direct line, or within the first or second degrees of the collateral line. They are likewise bound by the same obligation whenever they have been trustee or guardian to one of the parties before the court. This obligation binds here even if they are no longer connected with the person in the aforesaid capacity, the fact that they have been trustee or guardian in the past is sufficient to bring them under the meaning of this canon. The reason for the exclusion whether or not the trusteeship or guardianship has been relinquished, is based on the fact that these duties usually engender a certain bond of affection between the parties concerned, that cannot be regarded as ceasing with the legal termination of these duties.[59]

The three aforementioned officials are also to be excluded if they are connected by bond of intimate friendship with either or any of the parties before the court. The same rule also holds if ill-will exists between any of the parties and any of these officials. These officials, and the *Defensor* is included, may not act in a case in which they are likely to suffer great loss or gain, or in a case in which they have previously acted as either procurator or advocate.[60]

Since the basis for the exception of suspicion in all these cases,

[56] Canon 1613, § 2; Sipos, *Enchiridion,* p. 817; Noval, *De Processibus,* I, 118; Roberti, *De Processibus,* I, n. 156.

[57] Roberti, *De Processibus,* I, p. 248, n. 156.

[58] A Coronata, *De Processibus,* n. 1146, 1°.

[59] Roberti, *De Processibus,* I, 249; Noval, *De Processibus,* I, 196; Muñiz, *Procedimientos Eccles.,* III, 147.

[60] Canon 1613, §§ 1, 2,

is natural equity,[61] it would hardly seem reasonable to believe that all the causes justifying a recourse to the exception of suspicion are to be found in canon 1613, § 1. Any justifiable ground should in equity permit the acceptance of the exception of suspicion where well founded danger of prejudice is shown.

A distinction might be made here however, since the cases listed in canon 1613, § 1 are those in which both judge and *Defensor Vinculi* must abstain from action on their own initiative.[62] The conditions of the above canon must be considered to be listed taxatively inasmuch as the duty of both judge and *Defensor Vinculi* to abstain from a case for reasons other than those listed in the canon, would be at best doubtful and hence could give rise to no real obligation.[63] There is nothing, however, in either the above opinion or in canon 1613, to show that the exception in question could not be successfully urged against either the judge or the *Defensor Vinculi* on any grounds that would warrant the action.

In the event that this exception is raised against the *Defensor Vinculi* it must be alleged before the court and proven. The proof need not be very great, but of course it must convince the court.

The exception is heard and decided by the president of a collegiate tribunal. If there is only one judge hearing the case, he hears and decides the matter alone.[64]

The *Defensor Vinculi* cannot act in a case in which he appears as a witness, as he is excluded by canon 1757, § 3, 1°. It is also evident that the *Defensor* should not at the same time fill the position of the notary to the trial, or any other position in the trial in which he is acting as *Defensor Vinculi.*[65] To do so would certainly contravene the intention of the law, which wishes to remove all danger of personal prejudice or favor from coloring the actions of any of those officials of the court who act in the behalf of justice or the common good.

61 Wernz-Vidal, *Jus Canonicum,* VI, n. 146.

62 Canon 1613, § 1, " . . . ne suscipiat causam . . . "; § 2, " . . . ab officio suo abstinere debent . . . "

63 Roberti, *De Processibus,* I, 248.

64 Canon 1614, § 3; Muñiz, *Procedimientos Eccles.,* III, 147.

65 Roberti, *De Processibus,* I, 195.

In line with the foregoing provisions of the law is the prohibition imposed by canon 1624 on the judge or judges and all those assisting at the trial, forbidding them to accept gifts of any kind.[66] The law

[66] Noval, *De Processibus,* I, 130.

of this canon is more far reaching than the Pre-Code law, which permitted small presents such as things to eat and the like, but these are now forbidden. The prohibition is absolute, and is most reasonable, for nothing should be permitted that would tend to incline those assisting at the trial to one or the other party.

The offices of Promotor of Justice and *Defensor Vinculi* by express provision of the law may be held by the same person if the volume of work entailed is not too great.[67] In general the duties attached to these two offices are not incompatible, for they both seek to protect the common good, although in slightly different ways. It is possible, however, for the two offices to call for contradictory actions if they are held by the same person. Under these circumstances it would hardly be fitting for the two offices to be filled by the one and the same person,[68] who would be obligated to open the trial by attacking a marriage as invalid in his capacity as Promotor of Justice,[69] and also obliged to maintain the validity of the same marriage throughout the trial as *Defensor Vinculi.*[70]

It would not be legally consistent for the Vicar General, however, to hold the office of *Defensor Vinculi.* The Vicar General and the Bishop constitute in the eyes of the law, one person—the Ordinary.[71] As such he is the one by law given the right to appoint to the office of *Defensor Vinculi.*[72] The law has always implied that the incumbent in the office of *Defensor Vinculi* should be a person distinct from the Bishop, the local Ordinary. Consequently the Vicar General should not hold the office of *Defensor Vinculi,* nor should he appoint himself to the same office. If he were to do so, both judge and *De-*

[67] Canon 1588, § 1.

[68] Canon, 156, §§ 1, 2; Roberti, *De Processibus,* I, 196.

[69] Canon 1971, § 1, 2°.

[70] Canon 1968.

[71] Wernz-Vidal, *Jus Canonicum,* II, n. 545; Vermeersch-Creusen, *Epitome,* I, n. 366, 2.

[72] Canon 1589.

fensor Vinculi would be legally the same person. In addition, the grudging exception made by the law in canon 1588, § 1, permitting the same person to hold the offices of Promotor of Justice and *Defensor Vinculi* is a clear indication of the will of the lawgiver, showing an opposition to plurality of offices in so far as the office of the *Defensor Vinculi* is concerned.

Article IV

Preliminary Formalities

There are certain formalities that must be observed by the *Defensor Vinculi* before he actually takes up the work of his office.

The *Defensor Vinculi* appointed for all cases is obliged to take an oath of office at the beginning of his term and before he actually takes up his work.[73] This oath obliges him faithfully to fulfill his duties, without regard for the station in life of the persons involved, and with regard only for justice and the sanctity of the sacrament of Marriage.

This requirement is as old as the office itself, but the Code has made a minor change in the general law. Previously the *Defensor Vinculi* was obliged to take this oath every time he acted in a trial before the court.[74]

However the obligation in the present law of the Code is restricted to the time when he received his appointment if he is appointed for all cases.[75]

The obligation of the *Defensor Vinculi* to take this oath now has a double source in the Code, since it derives from both canon 364 and canon 1621. However the double source does not impose the obligation to take two oaths. If the *Defensor* takes the one oath on his appointment before the Bishop as a member of the Curia according to the demands of canon 364 he certainly fulfills the demands of canon 1621, which is supplementary inasmuch as it gives a more detailed description of the obligation, telling us that the minister of

[73] Canons 363, § 2, 1°, 2°; 364, § 2, 1°, 2°.

[74] Benedict XIV, const., *Dei Miseratione,* n. 7—*Fontes,* n. 318.

[75] Canon 1621, § 1, " . . . idque ab initio suscepti officii, si sint stabiles, . . . "

the court stably appointed merely has to take the oath once at the beginning of his term of office. This in the case of the *Defensor Vinculi* was a departure from the Pre-Code law.

The Bishop too, may include the obligation to secrecy within the content of the oath if he so wishes.[76]

The oath is taken before the Ordinary, who of course may delegate another priest to receive it in his stead, and of course the Vicar General may receive the oath.[77]

It will be noted that this oath is taken before the Ordinary who appoints to the office. If the office is filled only as the necessity arises, this *Defensor* appointed only for a special case has to take the oath as often as he is called before the court in a Matrimonial Trial.

With regard to the form of this oath, the essentials are laid down by the law of the Code; that is, there must be an invocation of the Divine Name, the priest touching the breast, all others touching a book of the Gospels.[78] Of course in addition to this, the oath must have been approved by the Ordinary or the *Officialis* who has full charge of the order of the trial.

In addition to the oath of office, the *Defensor Vinculi* is also obliged to make the Profession of Faith by virtue of the special law of the Motu Proprio of Pius X, *"Sacrorum Antistitum."*[79] This Motu Proprio, a special general law, imposes a double obligation, that is it imposes the obligation to take the Anti-Modernistic Oath in addition to the Profession of Faith according to the Formula of Pius IV with the Tridentine additions.[80] The Profession of Faith and the Oath are made before the Bishop or his delegate.[81]

This obligation as has been said before derives from a special general law. It is not part of the common law of the Church because it is temporary in nature. The law nevertheless binds the *Defensor*

[76] Canons 364, § 2, 3°; 1621, § 1.

[77] Canon 364, § 2, 1°; Roberti, *De Processibus,* I, p. 253, n. 160; Noval, *De Processibus,* I, 126.

[78] Canon 1622, § 1.

[79] September 1, 1910, Part IV—*Fontes,* III, n. 689, p. 783.

[80] Motu Proprio, Pius X, *Sacrorum Antistitum—Fontes,* n. 689, p. 783.

[81] S. C. Consist., Declar., September 25, 1910—*Fontes,* n. 2075.

Vinculi and the others that fall under it until revoked by the Holy See.[82]

Since the Profession of Faith is part of this obligation it cannot be made by proxy according to the Code,[83] a practice wholly in conformity with Pre-Code law.[84]

Article V

The Cases in Which the *Defensor Vinculi* Must Intervene

The *Defensor Vinculi* is a necessary party to all trials in which the validity or the nullity of a marriage is questioned during the lives of the parties to the marriage.[85]

Therefore whenever the validity of a marriage is impugned before the Ecclesiastical Court, the *Defensor Vinculi* must be cited, and this under pain of rendering the acts of the court null and void.

It is therefore the duty of the *Defensor Vinculi* to defend the bond of marriage, and it follows that if the validity of a marriage is attacked after the death of one of the parties, the bond no longer existing (having been dissolved by death), the *Defensor Vinculi* has no obligation to intervene in the case.

The *Defensor Vinculi* has the obligation to intervene in other cases than those which are being tried in the regular solemn process. He must intervene in the modified judicial process outlined in canons 1990 to 1992. In addition he is also obliged to act in the judicial investigation that must precede the grant of a Dispensation from a marriage that has never been consummated.[86] In this process he is

[82] *AAS,* X (1918), 136; Vermeersch-Creusen, *Epitome,* II, n. 740; Cance, *Le Code de Droit Canonique,* I, p. 40; *IER,* XI (1918), 429.

[83] Canon 1407.

[84] S. C. Concilii, *Valentina,* February 5, 1611—*Fontes,* n. 2387, " . . . Congregatio Concilii . . . censuit professionem fidei per procuratorem emitti nullo pacto potuisse . . ."; S. C. Concilii, *Caliguritana,* September 22, 1696—*Fontes,* n. 2954, " . . . ut novos provisos ad fidei professionem non admittat, nisi per se ipsos eamdem fidei professionem emittant."

[85] Canon 1586; Benedict XIV, const., *Dei Miseratione,* n. 6—*Fontes,* n. 318; S. C. S. Off., instr. (*ad Ep. Rituum Orient.*), a. 1883, Tit. II, n. 10, p. 397—*Fontes,* n. 1076.

[86] Canon 1967.

governed by the rules imposed by the instruction of the Sacred Congregation of the Sacraments.[87]

The *Defensor Vinculi* also must take part in the preliminary investigation which must precede all Matrimonial Cases in which the competence of the judge is based on quasi-domicile. This means that if the *Defensor Vinculi* must act in the main case, he must also act in this preliminary investigation.[88]

In all these cases the sanction of the law is the same. Whenever the presence of the *Defensor Vinculi* is required, if he was not cited the acta are invalid unless despite the lack of citation he was present at the sessions of the trial. If cited and absent from some sessions of the trial, the acta are valid, but must be submitted to the *Defensor* later so that he may correct or enlarge upon them if he thinks necessary. This he may do either orally or in writing.[89]

Some understand this canon to mean that if the *Defensor Vinculi* has been legitimately cited, he need not appear at the sessions of the trial at all, but merely to insure validity has to approve of them afterwards.

However to understand this canon to mean that the *Defensor* can be absent from all the sessions of the trial, and then approve the *acta* later if he were legitimately cited, seems to misinterpret the canon. The words *"aliquibus actibus"* cannot be given so wide an extension without doing violence to the essential meaning of the word *"aliquibus."*

Noval indeed dissents from this opinion, but it is interesting to note that he advances his opinion under the verb *"putamus,"* a confession that his opinion is by no means certain.[90]

It must be borne in mind however, that the question at issue is the required presence of the *Defensor Vinculi,* a condition required by the law under pain of nullity.[91] There can be no doubt that the failure to observe this condition imposed by the law would render

[87] *Catholica Doctrina,* May 7, 1923—*AAS,* XV (1923), 397; also S. C. de Sacram., *Normae,* March 27, 1929—*AAS,* XXI (1929), 490.

[88] Instr., S. C. de Sacr., December 22, 1929—*AAS,* XXII (1930), 168.

[89] Canon 1587, §§ 1, 2.

[90] Noval, *De Processibus,* n. 145; Sipos, *Enchiridion,* p. 812.

[91] Canon 1587, § 1.

the acta null and void.[92] It is also clear from other legislation that great value is placed on the actual presence of the *Defensor Vinculi* at certain phases of the trial, notably the hearing of the parties and witnesses, both because of the wording of the law and the extent of the privileges granted to the *Defensor Vinculi.*[93]

Consequently, granted the total absence of the *Defensor Vinculi* from the trial, despite any later approval on his part, it at least would be certain that he has not fulfilled his duties according to the prescriptions of the law.

The *Officialis* presiding over the trial would be rather unwise to permit such a situation to arise. In these matters it is better to follow the conservative advice given by Bouix under somewhat similar circumstances.

> Quo stante dubio, in praxi eiusmodi causas prudens iudex ecclesiasticus plenarii forma tractabit; ne forte, si qua in parte summarii processerit (quamvis adamussim servatis constitutionis Benedictinae praescriptionibus), processus ab aliqua partium, vel a matrimonii defensore, tanquam irregularis oppugnetur.[94]

He is in the case commenting on the advisability in those days of using a summary process under circumstances which seemed to him perfectly licit and valid, inasmuch as he felt the practice was not certainly abrogated by the const. *"Dei Miseratione"* of Benedict XIV.[95]

The obligation of the *Defensor Vinculi* to intervene in matrimonial trials where the validity of the marriage is questioned is quite obvious in most cases. However completeness demands that certain applications of the rule be given specific attention.

The *Defensor Vinculi* is a member of the Diocesan Curia, and his office demands that he fulfill his duties before the diocesan court. Hence, he is only bound to act when a marriage case is tried over

[92] Canon 1680, § 1.

[93] Canon 1968, § 1; *Regulae Servandae S. Romanae Rotae,* § 114, n. 12, "Testium examinibus interesse debet Defensor Vinculi. . . . "

[94] Bouix, *De Judiciis Ecclesiasticis,* II, 446.

[95] *Fontes,* n. 318.

which the Church has competence. Otherwise the ecclesiastical court would be incompetent to try the case. The Church however enjoys exclusive and native competence over the marriages of the baptized.[96] Whenever a marriage among baptized persons is called into question before the court the *Defensor Vinculi* is bound to act. There is no question about this, the obvious and ordinary case. It makes little difference whether the parties are Catholics or not. Even if both are non-Catholics and the Holy Office permits the marriage to be examined, the *Defensor* here too is bound by the full obligation of his office.[97]

If the marriage were contracted between a baptized non-Catholic and an unbaptized person, and if its validity were being examined by the ecclesiastical court with the permission of the Holy Office, the *Defensor Vinculi* is also obliged to act in the case, although it is probably only a legitimate marriage, and not sacramental in character.[98]

This distinction is not adverted to by either the law of the Code or the original law that founded the office of the *Defensor Vinculi Matrimonialis*.[99]

These cases are matrimonial cases and within the competence of the court. Consequently, whenever with the requisite permission of the Holy Office, their validity is contested before the court, the *Defensor Vinculi* should be cited to defend the marriage.[100]

Only those cases which fall under the headings listed in canon 1990 may be excepted from being tried by the solemn process and under all the provisions that rule matrimonial trials under the law of the Code. However the *Defensor* has special obligations and duties in this documentary process which will be fully explained at a further point in this treatment.

There is one other case that might easily be the subject of mis-

[96] Canon 1960; Conc. Trid., Sess. XXIV, *De Matrimonio*, c. 12; Gasparri, *De Matrimonio* (1932 edit.), I, n. 1234.

[97] Hilling in AKKR, CV (1925), 117.

[98] Gasparri, *De Matrimonio* (1932 edit.), I, n. 36.

[99] Canons 1586, 1967; Benedict XIV, const., *Dei Miseratione*, n. 6—*Fontes*, n. 318.

[100] Canon 1586, " . . . in quibus agitur de vinculo . . . matrimonii"; Benedict XIV, const. *Dei Miseratione*, November 3, 1741, n. 6—*Fontes*, n. 318.

understanding. That is the case in which the invalidity of the marriage is obvious and publicly known. This case if it does not fall under one of the exceptions listed in canon 1990 must be tried under the solemn matrimonial process, and the *Defensor* has the same strict obligation to intervene.[101]

This provision of the law does not work the great hardships that at first sight it seems to impose, for a notorious fact does not need proof.[102]

There is another case that is somewhat similar yet essentially different from the above case. This is the instance in which the law of the form of marriage has been totally neglected by persons certainly subject to it. In this case the Bishop may simply make a declaration with regard to the nullity of the attempted marriage without any judicial process of any kind, summary or solemn. Since a judicial form is not required, the *Defensor Vinculi* is not required to intervene.[103]

If the form were used, but with substantial defect, this does not apply. This substantial defect too can be notorious, but even in this case the solemn process must be used, and the *Defensor Vinculi* of course must intervene.[104]

In all other cases the *Defensor Vinculi* is free of any obligation to intervene imposed by the general law of the Church. He may have an obligation however arising from particular law in certain localities.[105]

Among such cases which are truly matrimonial causes, we may enumerate, the investigation of the *status liber*,[106] actions arising from canonical betrothal, actions for separations a *mensa et thoro*, permanent or temporary. In many of these cases while the *Defensor*

101 A Coronata, *De Processibus*, p. 420; Chelodi, *Jus Matrim.*, n. 174; Cappello, *De Sacrament.*, III, n. 874.

102 Canon 1747, 1º.

103 Pontifical Commission, October 6, 1919, ad 17, *AAS*, XI (1919), 476 ff; Chelodi, *Jus Matrim.*, n. 174; Gasparri, *De Matrimonio* (1932 edit.), II, n. 1282; A Coronata, *De Processibus*, p. 420, n. 1484.

104 Sipos, *Enchiridion*, 885; Wernz-Vidal, *Jus Canonicum*, V, p. 843, n. 705.

105 Sipos, *Enchiridion*, 878; Wernz-Vidal, *Jus Canonicum*, V, n. 694.

106 Linneborn, *Grundriss des Eherechts*, p. 191.

has no obligation arising from general law, he has in certain localities an obligation arising from particular law.

In none of the above mentioned cases is the validity of a contracted marriage questioned, and consequently the *Defensor Vinculi* has no obligation whatever to intervene arising from the general law. The same is true in regard to the Preliminaries to the use of the Pauline Privilege, for here too, the antecedent marriage is not questioned, but is merely dissolved.

CHAPTER III

THE *DEFENSOR VINCULI* IN THE FIRST OR PROBATORY PERIOD OF THE TRIAL

General Remarks

The general law that governs the activity of the *Defensor Vinculi* in the trial is to be found in canons 1968, 1969 and 1984. These canons are general in scope and application and apply to the whole ambit of the duties of the *Defensor Vinculi.* The Code not satisfied to define the duties of the *Defensor Vinculi* in these canons alone, expressly mentions him in a large number of canons to be found scattered through the whole of that part of the Code of Canon Law which falls under the title *De Judiciis.*

This study will follow the general plan of the trial as outlined in the Code, treating first however those general canons which govern the whole of the activity of the *Defensor Vinculi* before the court.

Article I

The Presence Required on the Part of the *Defensor*

The first section of canon 1968 which defines the duties of the *Defensor* expressly imposes on this official the duty of being present at the examination of the parties to the trial, the witnesses and the experts judicially called to give opinions in the case. The law of this, the first paragraph of canon 1968, of course should not be understood in the sense that the *Defensor* is only obliged to presence at those sessions of the trial in which either the parties, witnesses or official experts are being examined. The canon at this point merely wishes to accentuate the importance of his presence at these sessions. This is easily understood when one considers that the Code gives the *Defensor* the special right to inject new questions into the examination whenever they are prompted by disclosures made by the witness.[1]

Canon 1587, § 1, in giving the special procedure to be followed by a *Defensor* who has been cited to the trial and who has chanced to be absent from one or several sessions, clearly implies that the *Defensor* normally is obliged to be present at all the sessions. The *Defensor* in order to be able to enjoy the right to examine the *acta* after the session with the right of either approving them or suggesting changes or additions, must have received the citation of the court. If he failed to receive a judicial citation, and also failed to be present at the session, the *acta* are simply null and void.[2]

Citation certainly indicates that the law intends the *Defensor Vinculi* to be present at each session of the trial. Canon 1587 in addition does not apply to any particular part of the trial but to the whole of the process.[3] It is therefore quite clear that the Code imposes on the *Defensor* the duty to attend all the sessions of the trial in which his presence is required. In this, the present law of the Code is in absolute agreement with the Pre-Code law which imposed on the *Defensor* the duty of an active anad personal presence at the sessions of all matrimonial trials in which the validity of a marriage is impugned. This law is to be found in the constitution, *"Dei Miseratione,"* of Pope Benedict XIV [4] in the following words:

> Ad officium autem Defensoris Matrimoniorum huiusmodi, . . . eumque opportebit in quolibet actu judiciali citari, adesse examini testium, voce et scriptis matrimonii validitatem tueri, . . .

Other Pontifical Instructions likewise teach the same concept of the law.[5]

[1] Canon 1968, 1°.

[2] Canon 1587, §§ 1, 2.

[3] "Si legitime citati aliquibus actibus non interfuerint . . . "—Canon 1587, § 2.

[4] *Fontes,* n. 318.

[5] " . . . et omnia voce ac scriptis deducturum, . . . Praeterea hic defensor matrimonii citandus erit ad quaelibet acta, . . . "—S. C. C., Instr., August 22, 1840—*Fontes,* n. 4069; Smith, *Marriage Process,* p. 294, n. 673.

The fact that the law has always demanded personal and active presence on the part of the *Defensor* is also indicated by a passage taken from the instruction issued by the Sacred Congregation of the Holy Office to the Oriental Bishops in the year 1883.[6]

> Quod si ob peculiares circumstantias matrimonii defensor singulis actis interesse nequiverit, absoluto processu eadem ipsi tradantur, ut eas exarare queat animadversiones quas tuendae matrimonii validitati necessarias iudicaverit.[7]

This passage clearly and incontrovertibly shows that the alternative procedure, by means of which the *Defensor* may be absent from one or several of the sessions of the trial, is not to be adopted as a general practice or even for all the sessions of the trial, but is to be regarded solely as an extraordinary method of procedure designed to give the *Defensor* a little more freedom in the exercise of his office.

That this interpretation, by which is applied the old law of these two instructions and the *"Dei Miseratione,"* is justifiable, is most evident when one adverts to the content of canon 6, 2° or 3°.

The law that regulates the office of the *Defensor Vinculi* has suffered little change through the promulgation of the Code of Canon Law, except in matters of detail which do not touch any essential part of the office.[8] Hence whether recourse is had to the second or third sections of canon 6, the result is the same; the law in those parts that agree with the former law is to be interpreted in the same way as the old law, and according to the teaching of the approved commentators on the old law.[9]

These instructions given by the Sacred Congregation of the Council and the Holy Office are far better than the words of any

[6] This instruction was sent to the Bishops of the United States in the same year by the Sacred Congregation of the Propagation of the Faith under whose jurisdiction they were at that time. *Cf.* Gasparri, *De Matrimonio* (edit. 1932), II, n. 1233, p. 276.

[7] Tit. II, n. 11—*Fontes,* n. 1076.

[8] Gasparri, *De Matrimonio* (edit. 1932), II, n. 1253.

[9] "Canones qui ex parte tantum cum veteri iure congruunt, qua congruunt, ex iure antiquo aestimandii sunt"—Canon 6, 3°.

commentator, for they are explanations of the law, with the force of law.[10]

Article II

The Right of the *Defensor Vinculi* to See the *Acta* of the Trial

Canon 1969, the canonical summary of the rights of the *Defensor*, defines in its first section one of the rights of this official which is applicable to the whole of the trial. The canon here gives the *Defensor* the right to see and examine the *acta* of the trial at any time during its progress regardless of whether they have been opened to the opposing parties or not.

The question that immediately arises is what *acta* may the *Defensor* see? The *acta* of any trial are of two classes, the *acta processus* which consist only of those documents, judicial decrees and citations which refer to the form of the procedure, and the *acta causae* which refer to the merits of the particular case.[11]

It must be borne in mind that the testimony is generally not intercommunicated between the parties until after all the witnesses have been examined. The judge may delay this publication until certain proofs have also been produced if he sees fit,[12] but all proofs and testimony must be published before the discussion of the case may take place.[13]

This act of publication signifies that the judge gives to both parties by decree the mutual right to see all the testimony offered in the case.

If the right of the *Defensor* to inspect the *acta* were limited to the *acta processus*, he would merely be able to see those sections of the proceedings that have to do with the form of the trial, that is he could only inspect judicial decrees, citations and other like

[10] The instruction of 1883 is still the law governing matrimonial trials among Catholics of the Oriental Rites. *Cf.* Cappello, *De Sacramentis,* III, n. 877.

[11] Canon 1642, § 1; Wernz-Vidal, *Jus Canonicum,* nn. 198, 200; Roberti, *De Processibus,* I, p. 297.

[12] Canon 1782, §§ 1, 2.

[13] Canon 1858.

forms. He would not be permitted to see the questions asked, the answers given, nor even the documents offered in proof.

The first section of the canon apparently gives to the *Defensor* the right to see only the *acta processus.* Closer examination of the rights and duties of this official clearly indicates that the law does not intend so to limit this right of the *Defensor.*

That the *acta causae* are not really withheld from the *Defensor* is attested by the fact that when a cited *Defensor* is absent from a session of the trial, all the *acta* are to be sent for examination.[14] This fact coupled with the right of the *Defensor* to be present at all sessions of the trial is a positive indication that there is no limitation of his right to see the *acta.* This question could only arise in connection with the exercise of the right of the *Defensor* before the *publicatio processus.* The testimony received in the trial, however, is never kept from the *Defensor Vinculi.* He may be present at all times, he may interject new questions, and in the event of his absence all the *acta* are subject to his scrutiny.

The testimony of the parties and witnesses remains secret for only one reason, the avoidance of collusion which is clearly indicated by the content of canons 1781, 1786.[15]

The basis for this fear is certainly lacking when the one concerned is the *Defensor Vinculi,* whom the law requires to be a person of proven prudence and zeal for justice, and as carefully selected as the judges themselves.

Only one conclusion is possible since the other rights given to the *Defensor* destroy all the probability of the contention that the right of the *Defensor* to see the *acta* is limited to the *acta processus.*[16]

Although the second section of canon 1969 gives the *Defensor* the right to acquaint himself with all proofs and allegations entered by the parties so that he may contradict them if necessary, the second section of canon 1968 imposes on him the further particular obligation to inspect and assure himself of the authenticity of all documents entered in evidence. These two instances in the law are

[14] Canon 1587, § 2: "Si legitime citati aliquibus actibus non interfuerint, acta quidem valent, verum postea eorum examini subicienda omnino sunt . . . "

[15] Noval, *De Judiciis,* n. 500.

[16] Canon 1969, 1°.

sufficient in themselves to give him in effect the right to inspect the *acta causae*, even if the expression *acta processus* were to be received in its limited sense. Proofs and documents do not pertain to the *acta processus* under the strict meaning of this term, for they have reference to the merit of the particular case, and do not pertain alone to the form of the procedure.[17]

In view of the fact that the *Defensor* has both the right and duty to be present at all the sessions of the trial,[18] what possible reason could there be for denying him the right of access to all the *acta* of the trial? There can be but one answer to this question, that will be an admission that the *Defensor* has the right to see all the *acta* of the trial at any time without distinction.[19]

Article III

The *Defensor* in the Preliminary Stages of the Trial

Having examined the two foregoing general aspects of the work of the *Defensor*, the next step in logical order is to study his duties in connection with the presentation of the *libellus*.

This *libellus*, a petition requesting the service of the court in settling a doubtful matter, must be in writing excepting of course the case in which the petitioner is unable to write or is otherwise legitimately impeded.[20] In those cases where the petitioner makes his request orally, he does so in the presence of the judge and notary, which latter official reduces it to writing; the petitioner then approves this official written copy of his plea.[21]

Every trial must be opened by the presentation of a petition by the plaintiff,[22] who according to the terminology of Canon Law is

[17] Canon 1642, § 1; Wernz-Vidal, *Jus Canonicum*, VI, nn. 198, 200; Roberti, *De Processibus*, I, p. 297.

[18] Canon 1587, §§ 1, 2, in relation with canon 1968, and in the light of remarks made in the first article of this study.

[19] De Becker, *De Matrimonio* (edit. 1931), p. 277; Fourneret, *Le Mariage Chrétien*, p. 342.

[20] Canon 1707, § 1; Sipos, *Enchiridion*, p. 879.

[21] Canon 1707, § 3; Farrugia, *De Matrimonio*, n. 366.

[22] Canon 1706.

called the *actor*. He may be seeking relief on his own behalf, alone or in consort with others, or officially by virtue of an office on the behalf of the common good.[23]

The *actor* is so called because he prosecutes an action (*actio*). An *actio* in the technical canonical sense may be defined as the legal right to seek in court what is one's due, or the juridical exercise of the same right.[24] The *actor* therefore is the one who exercises this right in court (the plaintiff), and he does so by presenting to the judge a petition requesting the services of the court, with a brief statement of his case.

The *pars conventa,* the defendant, is the one against whom a judicial action is taken, or from whom something is sought by means of judicial sentence or decree.[25]

Marriage trials or causes may be opened only by certain persons, who alone have a right to petition the court to investigate doubts with regard to the status of the marriage. Among these are the married persons themselves, provided the party petitioning is a Catholic and was not the cause of the impediment that has rendered the marriage null. The only other person who can accuse a marriage as null to the Church Court is the Promotor of Justice, and then only when the impediment is based on a fact in itself public.[26]

After recognizing the petition, the court considers firstly whether the petitioner has a right to stand in court, and secondly whether the court itself enjoys jurisdiction over the question and person before it.

The next point is to consider whether the *libellus* fulfills all the requirements of the law, both in content and form. If suffering from any defect the *libellus* is to be rejected by the court giving at the same time the reasons for the rejection. If these defects are remediable, the *libellus* may be amended and presented again to the court.[27]

[23] A Coronata, *De Processibus,* n. 1169, p. 76.

[24] *Inst.,* IV, 6; *Dig.,* 7, 51, 44; Roberti, *De Processibus,* I, n. 27.

[25] A Coronata, *De Processibus,* p. 77, n. 1170, 2°.

[26] Canon 1971, §§ 1, 2; S. C. S. Off., Resp., January 27, 1928—*AAS* (1928), p. 75; P. C. I. C., Resp., March 12, 1929—*AAS* (1929), p. 171; Gasparri, *De Matrimonio* (edit. 1932), II, nn. 1260, 1269, 1270, 1271.

[27] Canon 1709, §§ 1, 2.

The question however that demands attention at this point is whether the *Defensor Vinculi* is obliged to be present at these proceedings. On the one hand the *Defensor* certainly has the right and the duty to be present at all the sessions of the trial,[28] but on the other hand it seems that he has no clear right or duty to be present at the reception of the *libellus* in first instance, because this action is not really part of the judicial trial.

The canon that governs the procedure for the presentation or the rejection of the *libellus* makes no mention of the *Defensor's* presence at this act, yet the same canon is very careful to order his presence when it gives the procedure for the recourse against the rejection of the *libellus* before the next instance.[29]

The next tribunal in the order of appeal receives the recourse, and hears the arguments for and against the rejection of the *libellus.* If the validity of a marriage is involved in the case it must also hear the *Defensor Vinculi,* and indeed should hear him after the others have been heard.[30] Having done this the tribunal should then quickly decide the question.[31]

At first glance if the presence of the *Defensor* were not required at the time of the presentation of the *libellus,* it might seem that the common good, and the validity of the sacrament were left unprotected during this stage of the proceedings. A moment's thought, however, quickly dissipates this fear, for it is quite evident that the sacrament is sufficiently protected by the required presence of the *Defensor* of second instance during the hearing of the recourse against the rejection of the *libellus.*

The Code while conceding that the *Defensor* may take up his duties without citation, nevertheless clearly indicates that his presence cannot be required until after he may be cited to take part in the trial.[32] Citation of course does not take place until after the *libellus* has been accepted.[33]

[28] Canon 1968, and Article I of this chapter.

[29] Canon 1709, §§ 1, 2—" . . . a quo audita parte, et promotore iustitiae aut vinculi defensore, quaestio reiectionis expeditissime definienda est"—C. 1709, § 3; Sipos, *Enchiridion,* p. 835; A Coronata, *De Processibus,* p. 145, n. 1238, 2°.

[30] Canon 1984, § 1.

[31] Canon 1709, § 3.

[32] Canons 1587, §§ 1, 2; 1967.

[33] Canon 1711, § 1; S. C. C. Instr., August 22, 1840—"Hisce praemissis,

Before this time the trial proper has not begun, for the case remains untouched (*res integra*) until the citations have been issued.[34]

Since the *Defensor* is to be cited, and since this cannot be done until the *libellus* has been accepted, he hardly can be bound to anticipate the act by appearing before he has received a citation. The presentation of the *libellus,* too, is not juridically a part of the trial. It is not a truly judicial act. Against the decree of the judge rejecting the *libellus* it will be noticed that a recourse is given and not an appeal.[35]

The *Defensor* is bound only to presence during the judicial acts of the trial, and is not bound to presence in non-judicial proceedings, except in cases mentioned expressly by the law.[36] The required presence of the *Defensor* also cannot be a doubtful obligation, too much depends on it, for his absence when required by law to be present, renders the judicial proceedings valueless. The Code and the former law too have been very careful on this score, and his duties are quite clearly indicated.

The presentation of the *libellus* is only a preliminary that must be observed at the beginning of the trial, it is not a part of the trial but a mere request to the court to start a trial. One of course cannot be cited legally to appear in a trial, which the court has not as yet opened.

It is therefore certain that it cannot be proven that the presence of the *Defensor* is required at the proceedings that surround the presentation of the *libellus.* If insisted on, the result is difficult to harmonize with the other laws that regulate the trial.

The *Defensor* therefore has no certain obligation to be present at the reception or the rejection of the *libellus* by the court of first

quoties aliquis coniugibus instantiam in scriptis porriget super nullitate matrimonii . . . "—*Fontes,* n. 4069; S. C. S. Off., Instr. (ad Ep. Rituum Orient.), a. 1883, Tit. II, n. 6—"Accusatione sic recepta, munus moderatoris actorum Episcopus vel ipse sibi assumet . . . "—*Fontes,* n. 1076; Roberti, *De Processibus,* I, p. 436, n. 288.

[34] Canon 1725, 1°; Noval, *De Judiciis,* p. 50.

[35] Sipos, *Enchiridion,* p. 835, footnote.

[36] Canons 1586, 1967.

instance. Consequently he has no obligation whatsoever to appear, for a doubtful obligation is no obligation at all. It must be kept in mind, however, that the *Defensor* of the second instance must be called in when that instance is hearing the recourse against the rejection of the *libellus* in first instance.[37] It is well also to keep in mind that the *Defensor* concerned in this hearing is the *Defensor* permanently attached to the court of second instance.[38]

Immediately upon the acceptance of the *libellus*, the judge may proceed to the issuance of the citations. The *Defensor Vinculi* if not present on his own initiative, is to be cited at the same time as the defendant (*pars conventa*).[39]

If the judge in question has been appointed by the Ordinary he is obliged to call in the *Defensor Vinculi* attached to the Curia,[40] or to seek the appointment of a specially designated *Defensor*.

A delegated judge appointed by the Holy See, however, is free to use either the *Defensor Vinculi* regularly attached to the Curia of the diocese in which he acts or one of his own selection unless otherwise limited in his rescript of delegation.[41]

Article IV

The *Defensor* in the Pre-Judicial Investigation That Must Precede the Opening of the Trial When Competence is Derived from Quasi-Domicile

There is one case, however, in which the *Defensor* does take part in a discussion appertaining to the reception of the *libellus*. This occurs when a petition seeking to have a marriage declared null is presented to a court whose competence to judge the case is based on the title of *quasi-domicile*.

Here, however, the *Defensor* is not regulated by the law of the

[37] Canon 1709, § 3.

[38] Canon 1709, § 3; Sipos, *Enchiridion*, p. 835; A Coronata, *De Processibus*, p. 145, n. 1238, 2°.

[39] Roberti, *De Processibus*, I, p. 436, n. 288; Canon 1712, § 1.

[40] Canons 1589, § 1; 1607, § 2.

[41] Canon 1607, § 1.

Code, but by the law of a rather recent instruction issued by the Sacred Congregation of the Sacraments.[42]

By this instruction the *Defensor* is obliged to appear and take part in a preliminary investigation which the Sacred Congregation has ordered to be made, whenever the competence of the court over a case involving the nullity of a marriage, is based on *quasi-domicile.*

The purpose of this legislation is to avert any danger of fraud on the part of those desirous of freeing themselves from a marriage not to their liking, by having their case tried in a place in which they are unknown, and where important witnesses perhaps could not properly be heard. The instruction very clearly puts the burden of averting this danger on both the judge and the *Defensor Vinculi.*[43]

The main headings under which the investigation is to be made are defined by the instruction. Both judge and *Defensor Vinculi* are bound to ascertain whether the title of *quasi-domicile* is truly legal, the reasons for bringing the case into the court of *quasi-domicile,* and the grounds upon which the nullity of the marriage is alleged.

The parties are also to be questioned as to what proofs and documents can be more easily produced in the court of *quasi-domicile.* In addition, information is to be obtained as to the truth of the petition and the proofs offered, from the Curias of both domicile and the place of the marriage. The instruction decrees that the case cannot be tried unless this information has been obtained and judged to be sufficient as well as satisfactory.

If the Ordinary of either domicile or of the place where the marriage took place finds that the *actor* is inspired by ulterior motives he will request that the case be turned over to his court. The court of *quasi-domicile* will then consider whether it should accede to this request.[44]

[42] S. C. de Sacram., Instr., December 23, 1929—*AAS,* XXII (1930), 168 ff.

[43] "I—Antequam officialis uniuscuiusque Curiae libellum admittat introductionis causae nullitatis matrimonii ob competentiam ex titulo quasi-domicilii advenarum, praesertim exterae alicuius nationis, causae delibatio, assistente sacri vinculi Defensore, facienda est super his, qui sequuntur articulis:"—S. C. de Sacram., Instr., December 23, 1929, I—*AAS,* XXII (1930), 168 ff.

[44] Instr. Cit., I, 1, 2, 3, 4, 5.

This pre-judicial investigation follows along the lines of a *causa incidens* [45] and the question is settled by a decree of the judge.[46] Nevertheless this does not destroy its judicial character, since the *causa incidens* also may be terminated by judicial decree as well as by interlocutory sentence.[47]

During this investigation the *Defensor* is ruled by the same law, has the same rights, as in the formal trial itself.[48] He is, of course, bound to furnish the judge with questions for the interrogation of the parties on the points mentioned in the first part of the instruction,[49] and is obligated to study the answers given by the parties, as well as the documents and other proofs adduced by them in proof of their good faith.[50]

It will be noticed that Section II of this instruction is nothing more than a summary of the rights and duties of the *Defensor Vinculi* as defined by the Code. It will be unnecessary, therefore, to discuss them further at this point inasmuch as the rights and duties of the *Defensor Vinculi* are fully treated in other parts of this study.

In this investigation the *Defensor* has the same rights in the calling and questioning of witnesses that he would have in any *causa incidens* that might occur in the course of the principal trial.[51] It is, therefore, most evident that the Sacred Congregation wishes the *Defensor* in this investigation to proceed in the same manner as in the probatory and deliberative stages of the formal trial.

The judge terminates this hearing by decree. If the judge accepts the case, and the *Defensor* is not satisfied that the decision is in conformity with the dictates of justice, he is empowered to make a demand that the case be sent, either to the Curia of domicile or to that of the place where the marriage occurred. He does this in writing, at the same time stating his reasons for the demand.[52] Of

[45] Instr. Cit., III.

[46] Instr. Cit., IV, 4.

[47] Canon 1840, § 1; Roberti, *De Processibus,* II, n. 397.

[48] Instr. Cit., II.

[49] Instr. Cit., I, 1, 2, 3, 4, 5; II, 1.

[50] Instr. Cit., II, 2.

[51] Instr. Cit., IV, 1.

[52] Instr. Cit., IV, 5.

course the parties to the action, too, are free to object in like manner, and they too, may present a written statement of their objections with substantiating documents if necessary.[53]

The *Defensor Vinculi* is not obliged by law to object to the acceptance of the case on the part of the judge, as in the case in which he appeals from the first sentence for nullity.

If the judge persists in his decision to try the case against the opposition of the *Defensor,* the said official, if still dissatisfied with the decision, shall take recourse to the Sacred Congregation of the Sacraments.[54] It is at this point that this procedure assumes its own particular form. The difference lies in the fact that recourse against the decision of the judge of the forum of *quasi-domicile* to try the case is not mandatory on the part of the *Defensor* and that the recourse is not made to the court of second instance, but directly to the Sacred Congregation. The obligation to make this recourse rests on the *Defensor* only when he is confident that the ends of justice will be better served if the case is tried by either the court of domicile or of the place where the marriage occurred. He has no obligation to make the recourse even after his written objections have been rejected by the judge if he no longer feels the case should go to one of the other Curias.

The court of second instance is likewise ordered to examine the *acta* of this preliminary investigation as often as it receives a case on appeal from the lower instance in which competence was derived through the title of *quasi-domicile.* The court of second instance is bound to do this in all of these cases with the exception of those in which the Sacred Congregation has intervened and approved the jurisdiction of the court of *quasi-domicile.* If after examination of these *acta* the *Defensor Vinculi* is not satisfied that the matter was well handled, he should refer the matter to the Sacred Congregation of the Sacraments for settlement.[55]

Here too, the obligation rests squarely on the shoulders of both the *Defensor* and the judge of second instance to insist on the investi-

[53] Instr. Cit., IV, 6.

[54] Instr. Cit., IV, 8.

[55] Instr. Cit., V, 1.

gation of this pre-judicial investigation by which the competence of the judge of *quasi-domicile* was approved.

If the *Defensor* of second instance should decide that the findings of this investigation in first instance were not well established, he is obliged to refer the matter to the Sacred Congregation of the Sacraments. Here, also the *Defensor* is not obliged to any mandatory action, since he does not refer the matter to the Holy See unless he feels that the case warrants it.[56]

The last section but one of the dispositive section of the instruction gives the law to cover the case which was introduced under the title of *quasi-domicile* before the issuance of the instruction.

The *Defensor* faced with this type of case, whether he is the *Defensor* in first instance trying an unfinished case, or the *Defensor* in second instance acting in a case under appeal, is bound to investigate the title of *quasi-domicile* from which the judge derived his competence, and to insure himself that the parties were not moved by motives fraudulent in nature. He is not bound to observe all the minutiae of this instruction, but only to assure himself, that the general purpose of the instruction, the avoidance of fraud is insured.[57]

The *Defensor* in handling these pre-judicial investigations is bound in conscience to refer the matter to the Sacred Congregation of the Sacraments, in every case in which he cannot remove all suspicion of fraud on the part of the parties seeking to have their case tried in the court of *quasi-domicile.*[58]

The final section of the instruction places the same obligations on the *Defensores* of third and further instances.[59]

It is well to notice that the *Defensor* in these hearings acts in the same manner, and with the same rights that he would have in an incidental case. He petitions the calling of witnesses, presents his questions closed and sealed to the judge for use in the examination, scrutinizes documents, and finally must declare he has concluded his

[56] Instr., V, 1.

[57] " . . . quae in Domino ei magis expedire videantur, pro gravitate sui officii, . . . "—Instr. Cit., V, 2.

[58] Instr. Cit., V, 2.

[59] Instr. Cit., V, 3.

case before the hearing may be closed.[60] This done, the *Defensor* presents the defense of his position in the case, a proceeding similar to the *discussio causa* of the solemn trial.[61]

The *Defensor* is under no obligation to insist always that the case be tried in the Curia of domicile or of the place where the marriage occurred, but rather to make certain that the court of *quasi-domicile* is not being selected for reasons tinged with fraud and deceit. If it is his opinion, that the court of *quasi-domicile* is not the proper court to try the case, then he is bound in conscience to insist that the case be tried in one of the other competent Curias, and meeting with refusal on the part of the judge to accede to this request, he is then bound in conscience to refer the matter to the Sacred Congregation of the Sacraments for settlement.[62]

The *Defensor* acting in these investigations must bear in mind that the judge has an obligation to prevent these hearings from becoming too long or involved.

The principal case is not under investigation at this point, and its merits may be considered only in so far as they will evidence the good faith of the *actor* in selecting the forum of *quasi-domicile.* Therefore, a certain moderation must be observed in the number of witnesses called, and in the amount and extent of the proofs. The judge consequently is obliged to restrain the *Defensor* if he is inclined to be unreasonable in this regard.

The judge must, however, hear the *Defensor* before the *conclusio in causa* is decreed, but he need not yield to him, unless he feels that the objections of the *Defensor* are based on solid grounds.

The side of the *Defensor* is not really weakened by an adverse decision from the judge at this point, for if dissatisfied with the decision of the judge, he may always make the necessary recourse to the Holy See; in fact he is bound in conscience to do so, if he believes it to be useful or necessary.

[60] Instr. Cit., IV, 3.
[61] Instr. Cit., IV, 4.
[62] Instr. Cit., IV, 5, 8.

Article V

The *Defensor Vinculi* in the Probatory Sessions of the Trial

A. *The Rights of the "Defensor" in the Calling of Witnesses*

The duty of presence on the part of the *Defensor* in that portion of the trial in which the proofs and evidence are collected is not fulfilled by mere presence. On the contrary the whole brunt of the work of these sessions falls on the *Defensor Vinculi* and he is obligated to a most active participation in these proceedings if he is to fulfill his duties properly.

The general statement in the law that must guide him in this part of the trial is to be found in canon 1968, 1°. Here the duty is imposed on him to be present at the examination of the parties, witnesses and experts, to present to the judge questions for the interrogation of those to be examined. In addition he enjoys the right to suggest new additional questions to the judge as often as they are prompted by the findings of the examination.

The greater part of the proofs used in formal marriage trials is derived from the testimony given by the parties, witnesses, and experts called to testify in the case.[63] Hence the calling and the examination of both parties and witnesses is a most important part of the trial.

Witnesses may be called to testify in matrimonial cases, by both parties and *Defensor Vinculi*.[64]

In general the production of witnesses runs along the following lines. The party who is calling the witnesses directs a petition to the judge giving the names of his witnesses in full, as well as their places of residence. He also includes in the petition *positiones*, affirmative statements to be used as the basis of questions, or prepared lists of questions, with which he wishes the judge to question his witnesses and those of the opposing party.[65]

[63] Payen, *De Matrimonio*, III, p. 500, § 3, 1°.

[64] Canon 1759, § 2; A Coronata, *De Processibus*, p. 199, n. 1288, 2°, Sipos, *Enchiridion*, p. 843.

[65] Canon 1761, §§ 1, 2; Roberti, *De Processibus*, II, n. 339.

In former times these question forms had a very definite format. Forms called *positiones* were used, which were short and simple narratives of fact, and which were introduced by one party to be proposed to the other party for the purpose of seeking affirmation or denial. Affirmation would be judicial confession.[66] Their name is derived from their affirmative character. They were proposed only to the opposing parties, for the purpose of drawing up the *articuli,* which were statements of the facts that were controverted.[67]

These forms are no longer observed and question lists are now submitted for the questioning of both parties and witnesses alike. These are lists of simple brief questions designed to show, first the identity of the witness, and then disclose the information which he is believed to possess. These questions must not be leading, captious or of a type intended merely to trap the witness into an admission without realizing what he is saying.[68]

In the event that an involved and complicated marriage case should appear before the court, in which the petition of the *actor* does not clearly define the points at issue, the judge may cite the parties before the court, either *ex officio* or at the instance of either party or of the *Defensor Vinculi,* in order that the points at issue may be clarified. This procedure is called the *concordantia dubiorum.* The *Defensor* has the right to demand it if he thinks it to be necessary or useful.[69] From this discussion the articles of the controversy are formed, and they cannot be changed during the trial except for grave cause and by decree of the judge, at the instance of either one of the parties or of the *Defensor.* In this procedure the other party must always be heard, as well as the *Defensor,* before the issuance of the decree making the desired change.[70]

However, this will occur but rarely in matrimonial trials of

[66] A Coronata, *De Judiciis,* p. 172, n. 1268, 2°.

[67] A Coronata, *De Judiciis,* p. 172, n. 1268, 2°; Roberti, *De Processibus,* II, p. 321.

[68] Canon 1775; Roberti, *De Processibus,* II, p. 21, n. 321.

[69] Canon 1728; *Reg. Servandae S. R. Rotae,* § 33, n. 2; Noval, *De Judiciis,* p. 293, n. 414.

[70] Canon 1729, § 4, Wernz-Vidal, *Jus Canonicum,* VI, n. 402.

nullity, for the question under controversy will usually be rather simple, though the proof of the simple fact of nullity may be most involved.

The parties to the trial have the obligation to make the names of their witnesses known to each other. This should be done ordinarily by giving this information to the court which will in turn transmit it to the other parties. However, if this cannot be done without great inconvenience, or if there is danger of reprisals or fraud on the part of the other party, the judge according to his own prudent judgment may delay this exchange of the names of the witnesses until just before the *publicatio processus*.[71] The names are interchanged in order that the parties may have an opportunity to have objectionable witnesses excluded. They have the right to seek the exclusion of witnesses within the three days following the communication of the names of the witnesses. They cannot exercise this right after the three days have elapsed unless they can show or affirm by oath that the defect on the part of the witness was not previously known to them.[72]

It is, therefore, to enable the parties to exercise this right that they are obliged by the law to exchange the names of their respective witnesses. The disqualification of a witness is known in Canon Law as *reprobatio*, and this right must be exercised by the opposing party within the three days following the communication of the names of the witnesses.[73]

The *Defensor* having the right to have witnesses called may exercise all the other rights enjoyed by the parties in this connection. He, too, can seek the disqualification of a witness. This is an evident conclusion that must be derived from his general grant of power in canons 1968 and 1969.[74]

In order to confirm more certainly this right of the *Defensor*

[71] Canon 1763; Roberti, *De Processibus*, II, n. 339.

[72] Canon 1764, § 4; Noval, *De Judiciis*, p. 336.

[73] Canon 1764, § 4.

[74] "Defensori vinculi jus esto: . . . 3° Petere ut alii testes inducantur. . . . "—Canon 1969, 3°; " . . . eaque omnia deduce, quae ad matrimonium tuendum utilia censuerit"—Canon 1968, 3°.

it is necessary to mention the express declaration of the power in canon 1759, § 2.[75]

The real question at issue is, does the *Defensor* have to inform the parties of the names of his witnesses? Considering the purpose of the law it would seem indeed that he does. This purpose is to enable the parties to seek the disqualification of witnesses that are not legally acceptable. The *Defensor* is an official of the Curia, he is not personally involved or acquainted with the people involved, and he cannot know the witnesses very well, either in their background or their character. It could very readily happen that one of these witnesses might be laboring under a very deep seated and unprincipled prejudice against one of the parties, the hearing of whose testimony would work grave injustice on the subject of his ill will.

This argument is not so strong as it seems. The party will learn of the identity of the witness at the publication of the testimony. He will then have for three days the right to seek his disqualification, and so the ends of justice will be protected.

The mere fact that the *Defensor* is not mentioned in canon 1763, neither confirms nor denies his obligation to disclose the names of his witnesses. The broad powers given to the *Defensor* in canons 1968 and 1969 almost seem to make out a presumption of freedom for the *Defensor*. He enjoys a favored position throughout the whole trial, he may be present at all the sessions, may interject additional questions into the examination and is entitled to speak last, not to mention several other important rights granted to him by canons 1968 and 1969. This predominance of privilege enjoyed by the *Defensor Vinculi* though it may seem to give him an unfair advantage over the parties, discloses itself differently when it is realized that the qualifications of the *Defensor* are the same as those demanded in the judge himself, for the Code demands that the *Defensor* too, be trustworthy and zealous for justice.[76]

The parties do not lose their right to seek the disqualification of a witness regardless of at what stage of the trial they learn his identity. They still retain the right to seek the rejection of the wit-

[75] Canon 1759, § 1, Testes a partibus inducuntur; § 2, Possunt quoque induci a promotore justitiae et defensore vinculi, si id ad causam intersit."

[76] Canons 1589, 1573, § 4; 1613, §§ 1, 2.

ness for three days after they learn his identity, for canon 1764 § 4, in no way distinguishes or limits the right, giving only one condition, the exercise within three days of the communication of the names of the witnesses. The parties consequently suffer no disability.

It must be concluded then that the *Defensor Vinculi* has no real obligation to disclose the names of his witnesses before the *publicatio processus*. His own prudence and wisdom will, however, dictate that at times he should disclose these names at the same time that the parties do so in order to expedite the progress of the trial, especially in those cases in which he is the only one on the side of validity. This conclusion derives from the fact that the Code places the obligation to interchange the names of the parties to the trial.[77] The *Defensor Vinculi* while he acts after the fashion of a party, is not a party to the trial in the strict sense. A party to an action cannot act *ex officio*, the *Defensor* cannot act otherwise.

B. *The Order in Which the Witnesses Are to Be Heard*

The order in which the witnesses are to be called and examined may be regulated by the judge. The witnesses of the *actor* (plaintiff) ought to be heard first, unless reasonable cause dictates another order. After the witnesses of the plaintiff, those appearing for the defendant (*pars conventa*) ought to be examined, and finally those called by the *Defensor* ought to be heard last. Witnesses called by the Promotor of Justice, ought to be heard before those called by the *Defensor Vinculi* and after those of the parties to the trial.[78]

Reasonable cause will justify the judge in departing from the above order. Practically these hearings are arranged so as to keep the witnesses apart, and thus prevent them from approaching the place of the hearings at about the same time. This is a wise procedure dictated both by the canonical legislation forbidding any intercommunication between the witnesses and parties, and also by the fact that great ill-feeling is often engendered by marital difficulties. The greater convenience to the witness too, will also justify the

[77] Canon 1763.

[78] Muñiz, *Procedimientos Eccles.*, III, n. 297; Smith, *The Marriage Process*, p. 95, n. 192; Smith, *Elements*, II, n. 1469.

arranging the time so that he may appear before the Curia without losing time from work, or suffering other unwarranted inconvenience or expense.

C. *Special Rights Enjoyed by the "Defensor" in the Calling of Witnesses*

In general witnesses may be called at any time in the trial up to the *publicatio processus,* when the judge by decree gives both sides the right to see the testimony that was given in the trial.[79] At this point the normal period for the production of witnesses and the gathering of evidence is closed, for the parties and the *Defensor* have indicated that they have nothing further to bring to the attention of the court.

In marriage trials, since the status of the marriage is involved, simple grave reason is sufficient to justify the judge in permitting the parties to bring in witnesses even after the *publicatio processus.* The judge must also be sure that all danger of fraud and subornation is removed. In addition, before he does this he must give the other party and the *Defensor Vinculi* an opportunity to interpose whatever objections they may have to the admission of witnesses at this stage of the trial.[80]

The *Defensor* on the other hand, has a more substantial right to call witnesses at any time in the trial, and to seek the reexamination of witnesses, since for this he needs no grave cause, but may do so as long as he believes the procedure to be useful.[81]

This right is granted to him by the law itself, independently of the general principle found in canon 1786, which declares that after the testimony collected in the trial has been declared accessible to the contending parties, that witnesses already examined may not be reexamined again on the same *articuli* nor may new witnesses be admitted except under the conditions placed by the law.

By the word *articuli,* here is meant the general statements of fact

[79] Canon 1860, §§ 2, 3; Roberti, *De Processibus,* II, p. 67.

[80] Canon 1786; Sipos, *Enchiridion,* p. 846; A Coronata, *De Processibus,* p. 220, n. 1312, 2°.

[81] Canon 1968, 3°.

upon which the questions put to the witness are based; they, therefore, are simple statements of the controverted fact or facts, upon which the judge is to apply the law.[82]

In making use of this right the *Defensor* has the obligation to make certain that all danger of fraud and corruption is removed when he calls in a witness after the *publicatio processus.* This obligation derives not from any specific canon, but rather from the purpose of his office, the safeguarding of truth and justice.

After the *publicatio processus* both parties to the marriage trial may seek the reexamination of witnesses or the calling of new ones, provided they first convince the judge that there is grave reason for so doing. The judge must be certain that there is no danger of fraud in connection with the witness called so late in the trial. He must also have given the other party and the *Defensor* an opportunity to interpose objections. He then admits the witness by decree, and he should mention in the decree that the above formalities of the law have been observed.[83]

It will be noticed that the right of the *Defensor* is a twofold one, both to recall and reexamine witnesses already heard, and to call new witnesses after the *publicatio processus* as well.

He brings the witnesses into court in the usual manner, by requesting the judge to call them. The *Defensor,* however, may be denied this request only on the unanimous vote of the judges.[84]

The law itself clearly indicates that the only reason for the restriction placed on the calling of witnesses after the *publicatio processus,* is the avoidance of the possibility of fraud and collusion. The *Defensor* is not hampered by these restrictions since he has been chosen according to law with the same care with which the judge was chosen. He, however, has no right to delay the trial unduly, and hence his action would be unjustified if he were to call witnesses after the *publicatio processus* who could just as readily have been called at the customary time.

[82] Roberti, *De Processibus,* II, p. 21.
[83] Canon 1786.
[84] Canon 1969, 4°.

Article VI

The *Defensor Vinculi* and the Examination of the Parties and the Witnesses

Both parties have the right to submit to the judge either *positiones* or questions with which they wish the other party and the witnesses to be questioned.[85] These *positiones,* positive statements of fact are little used now, and the word is often used loosely to mean a list of prepared questions. The common practice today is to present a prepared set of questions.[86]

The *Defensor,* may if he so desires, submit brief positive statements of fact (*positiones*), but in addition he must also submit prepared lists of questions, to be used by the judge in the examination of the witnesses and parties. The law places special safeguards about these questions, for they are a most important part of the work of the *Defensor.* The questions must be submitted to the court by the *Defensor Vinculi,* closed and sealed, and are to be opened by the judge only in the act of examination itself.[87]

These questions consequently must be specially prepared for each person to be examined, and enclosed in separate envelopes. The questions both in form and matter should conform to the general requirements of the law concerning the questions used in the trial.[88]

The judge in examination should use the questions of the *Defensor Vinculi* after he has completed the examination with the questions proposed by the parties to the trial. In the event that the Promotor of Justice should happen to be active in the trial, his questions should be proposed immediately before those of the *Defensor Vinculi* and after those of the parties.[89]

[85] Canon 1745, § 1; Sipos, *Enchiridion,* p. 840.

[86] A Coronata, *De Processibus,* p. 172, n. 1268, 2°; Roberti, *De Processibus,* II, pp. 20, 21.

[87] Canon 1968; *Regulae S. R. Rotae,* n. 114, 3°; Sipos, *Enchiridion,* p. 878; A Coronata, *De Processibus,* p. 421, n. 1484.

[88] Canon 1775; Sipos, *Enchiridion,* p. 845.

[89] Canon 1984, § 1.

This order is subject to change for any reasonable cause. The questions of the *Defensor Vinculi* are often more suitable and hence frequently used in the first place. In fact the *Regulae Servandae* for the *Ratum et non consummatum* process seem to imply that this is the regular practice in that investigation.[90] The instruction of 1883 also seems to imply that the questions of the *Defensor Vinculi* should be used before the questions of the parties.[91]

This, a minor detail in the law, is therefore somewhat doubtful, and at the same time of no great practical importance. Regardless of whether the questions of the *Defensor Vinculi* are used in first or last place, he always maintains the right to interject questions whenever he believes them to be necessary.[92]

The *Defensor* at the same time has the general right to be present throughout these examinations. Coexistent with this right is his other right to interject new questions into the examination as often as he sees fit.[93] He does not ask these questions himself, but submits them to the judge who then puts them to the witness.[94]

It is just at this point that the implications of the law cannot clearly be discerned. May the judge change the questions of the *Defensor Vinculi?* Of course, minor and obviously necessary changes will offer no difficulty, such as the correction of obvious errors. But can the judge substantially change or omit a whole question?

The safeguards with which the Code protects these questions would seem to indicate that the answer should be negative. The questions are delivered to the judge in a closed and sealed packet or envelope. Why this precaution? Why are they kept from the judge until the moment that he is ready to use them? Evidently it is the wish of the legislator to protect these questions in every possible way. Would the judge not be permitted to read these questions before

[90] *Reg. Serv. Super Rato,* n. 50, § 1.

[91] S. C. S. Off., Instr. (*ad Ep. Rituum Orient.*), a. 1883, Tit. III, n. 18—*Fontes,* n. 1076.

[92] Canon 1968, 1°.

[93] Canon 1968, § 1; A Coronata, *De Processibus,* p. 421, n. 1484.

[94] Canon 1773, §§ 1, 2; *Regulae S. R. Rotae,* n. 114, 5°; A Coronata, *De Processibus,* p. 421, n. 1484, p. 214, n. 1303, 3°; Sipos, *Enchiridion,* p. 845; Fourneret, *Le Mariage Chrétien,* p. 346.

the interrogation, if he were empowered to change them? The law, however, clearly states that these questions are to be opened in the very act of examination and not before.

It is indeed true that the judge presides over the trial and that he has certain rights and duties connected with his moderatorship.[95] He is bound, for instance, to keep the examination both in length and scope within the bounds of reason.

On the other hand the extensive rights enjoyed by the *Defensor* almost seem to make out for him a presumption of freedom.[96] He is given the fullest opportunity to do everything in his power which he believes that justice demands of him in the protection of the sacrament of Marriage. The *Defensor* is really bound by but one restriction which permits his motion to be rejected by unanimous action of the judges.[97]

The practice enforced by the Code seems to indicate a desire to give protection to these questions. It must be kept in mind that both the judge and the *Defensor,* seek to protect the public good, and there really ought to be little room for friction on this score.

If unfortunately a dispute should arise on this point, the *Defensor* may seek relief in the manner outlined by canon 1625, § 1, and failing in this he may, of course, attack the proceeding in the *libellus* which shall accompany his appeal in the event of a sentence declaring the marriage null.

The *Defensor,* while highly privileged, is nevertheless under the authority of the judge, who alone is responsible for the proper handling of the case as a whole. It is his duty to prevent the trial from becoming too long or unnecessarily involved, and hence he has the right to exclude questions that are useless or offensive.[98]

[95] Canon 1762.

[96] Vermeersch-Creusen, *Epitome,* III, p. 128, n. 283.

[97] Vermeersch-Creusen, *loc. cit.*

[98] Canon 1775; *Regulae S. R. Rotae,* n. 148; Roberti, *De Processibus,* II, p. 62.

Article VII

The *Defensor Vinculi* and the Written Depositions of the Parties and the Witnesses

The notary of the court must make a written record of all that occurs during the trial. This includes anything worthy of mention, and an exact account of the questions and answers given and received during the examination. This written record of the examination must be read to the witness before he leaves the place of examination. The witness must also be given the opportunity to change, suppress, or correct his testimony. This done he signs the written record of his testimony which is signed in turn by the judge and the notary.[99] This is the general law for the conduct of an examination in a contentious trial. When the case concerns the nullity of a marriage, the required presence of the *Defensor Vinculi* gives rise to some speculation as to what the procedure should then be.

Canon 1779 embodies the general law that should guide the notary in making his written record of the court proceedings.[100]

Judicial practice has given a very definite form to the meaning of this canon. The official written record of the case, the *acta* should give the general references that identify the case, which should appear on each folio or sheet of the *acta,* as well as its number, for the pages of the record must be consecutively numbered. It is the general practice also to indicate the Curia which is trying the case.

Each court will have its own particular format, but all will agree in essentials, and this particular format should be followed, whether it is fixed by custom, or positive regulation of the Curia itself.

In addition to the invocation of the Divine Name, the date and the place, the introductory part of the *acta* should also disclose the full names of the judge, judges or auditor presiding, the name of the *Defensor Vinculi,* as well as that of the Promotor of Justice if he

[99] Canon 1780, §§ 1, 2; Roberti, *De Processibus,* II, p. 65.

[100] Canon 1779—"Actuarius in actis mentionem faciat de praestito, remisso aut recusato iureiurando, de partium aliorumque praesentia, de interrogationibus ex officio additis et generatim de omnibus memoria dignis quae forte acciderint, cum testes excutiebantur."

is acting in the case. Essential also is the name of the notary charged with keeping the record of the proceedings.[101]

This is the general form that is followed by many courts, and it will be noticed that it indicates the presence of all those required for the validity of the session.

In the record of the examination, the origin of the questions used should also be indicated, and hence the questions entered by the *Defensor* should be so credited to him in the *acta* as well as the fact that they were received closed and sealed, and opened in court according to the requirements of the law. Most of these formalities will be followed automatically and as a matter of course. It frequently happens that these questions are presented to the court by depositing them with the notary. If this is the case the judge ought to authorize the notary by decree to open them at the proper time.[102] This decree, of course, must be entered in the *acta*. The presence of this decree and the note of its execution in the official record of the trial certainly will be sufficient notice that the law has been observed.

The *Defensor* in addition has the right to inject other questions into the examination as often as he feels them to be either useful or necessary.[103] Such questions may be proposed by the *Defensor Vinculi* at any time during the course of the hearing, and should be duly accredited to him in the *acta*. This may be done in a variety of ways, since each court has its own individual practice for the regulation of the smaller details of the trial. These questions are the *ex officio* questions of the *Defensor Vinculi* and they usually bear this caption in the *acta*.[104]

Some doubt attaches itself to the necessity of the *Defensor Vinculi* affixing his signature to the written record of the testimony at the end of the hearing. A double question presents itself. May the *Defensor* licitly sign these depositions? Is he obliged by the law of the Code to do so?

The *Defensor* certainly was obliged to sign these depositions by the law in force prior to the promulgation of the Code of Canon Law.

[101] Roberti, *De Processibus*, II, n. 349.

[102] Santi, *Praelectiones J. C.*, lib. IV, p. 154, n. 32.

[103] Canon 1968, 1°.

[104] Roberti, *De Processibus*, II, n. 349.

The Pre-Code law on this point is to be found chiefly in two instructions of the Holy See, the one issued by the Sacred Congregation of the Council in 1840 [105] and the other by the Holy Office in the year 1883.[106]

The first instruction, that of 1840, is quite explicit:

> Deinde ipse (testis) subscribit, et, si fuerit illiteratus, per signum crucis; dein iudex et defensor validitatis matrimonii apponent suam subscriptionem, et cancellarius de actu rogabit.[107]

The later instruction sent by the Holy Office to the Orientals, and in the same year, 1883, sent by the Sacred Congregation of the Propagation of the Faith to the Bishops of the United States, is equally explicit:

> . . . deinde ipse examinatus subscribat, et si fuerit illiteratus, faciet hoc signum crucis; ac denique moderator actorum et defensor validitatis matrimonii apponent suam subscriptionem, et cancellarius de actu rogabit.[108]

As in the original law of the office of the *Defensor Vinculi*,[109] so in the new Code of Canon Law, the rights and duties of the *Defensor Vinculi* are frequently indicated in a general way.[110] The specific application of these rights and duties is not made by the law in every instance. In certain sections of the general law of the trial found in the Fourth Book of the Code there is to be found particularized applications of the law of the *Defensor Vinculi*, but such treatment is not complete.

However, the two aforementioned Roman instructions give an official interpretation of a law that seemingly has not been changed by the Code. The Code merely restates the law that regulates the

[105] *Fontes*, n. 4069.

[106] *Fontes*, n. 1076.

[107] S. C. C. Instr., August 22, 1840—*Fontes*, n. 4069.

[108] S. C. S. Off., Instr. (*ad Ep. Rituum Orient.*), a. 1883, n. 14—*Fontes*, n. 1076; Gasparri, *De Matrimonio* (edit. 1932), II, p. 276.

[109] Benedict XIV, Const., *Dei Miseratione*, November 3, 1741—*Fontes*, n. 318.

[110] *Cf.* CC. 1968, 1969, 1586, 1590.

actions of the *Defensor*. Some changes are made, but they are merely minor ones, and small in number. The office of the *Defensor Vinculi* has suffered only slight change from the time of its foundation to the present day. Therefore it would seem that one may go to the Pre-Code law without the slightest hesitation in order to discern a proper method of action for the *Defensor*.

To do so would be to act in perfect conformity with canon 6, which in its third section gives us a rule making allowances even for the almost negligible changes made in the law that governs the office of the *Defensor Vinculi*. The third section of this canon reads as follows:

> 3° Canones qui ex parte tantum cum veteri iure congruunt, qua congruunt, ex iure antiquo aestimandi sunt; qua discrepant, sunt ex sua ipsorum sententia diiudicandi.

The changes in the law that regulates the *Defensor Vinculi* are few and unimportant. They are merely changes in the application of the law, as for example, the *Defensor* before the Code was obliged to take the oath of office every time he began a case, now if he is permanently appointed, he is obliged to take the oath only when he enters into office.

Section 4° of the same canon also has some application to the present question. It reads:

> In dubio num aliquod canonum praescriptum cum veteri iure discrepet, a veteri iure non est recedendum.

What then is the status of the law at present with regard to the necessity of the *Defensor's* signature to the depositions? There is a general statement of the law in the Code, with no specific application to the point under discussion. In the old law there are two instructions, official instructions, that were laws in the strict sense of the word. These laws give the exact application of the law to the point in question. There is no disagreement with the old law, hence the law as explained in the past is still effective. According to canon 6, 4° there is really no room for doubt.

The doubt centers about the opinion that this requirement is superfluous.[111] But is it really superfluous? In many cases it is actually useless. This is particularly so when the *Defensor* has been active in the case, and the record of the examination is well sprinkled with his *ex officio* questions. Outside of this instance, however, it does not seem to be a useless formality of the law, since after the *Defensor* presents his prepared list of questions to the court, there is no other proof that he was actually present during the examination itself. There is indeed proof if the notary has noted at the opening of the examination of the witness in question that the *Defensor* was present, but if this notice is to be found at the beginning of the *acta* of a session during which several witnesses were heard, there is no assurance that the *Defensor* was present during every moment of the trial. It is quite possible that the *Defensor* might have slipped away for a few moments and the examination of a witness might have taken place in the interim during which he was actually absent. If this were so, the record would not indicate the true state of affairs.

If the *Defensor* signs the deposition of the witness this is most certain proof that he really and actively was present during the hearing. It will also serve to inform the court trying the case on appeal, that the *Defensor* was carefully fulfilling his duties.

Hence it seems clear that this formality is not entirely a useless one, since under certain circumstances it will serve to indicate that the *Defensor* was actually present, when otherwise his presence would be doubtful.

Did the Holy See intend to eliminate this requirement of the law? The new instruction issued by the Sacred Congregation of the Propagation of the Faith recently sent to China under the date of February 18, 1929, for the regulation of matrimonial trials does not eliminate it, for it repeats word for word in its section 14, the wording of section 14 of the instruction of 1883, then sent to the Oriental Bishops and the Bishops of the United States.[112]

Likewise the *Regulae Servandae,* issued by the Sacred Congregation of the Sacraments to govern the investigation that must be made before the grant of dispensation from a nonconsummated marriage,

[111] Roberti, *De Processibus,* II, p. 65, footnote 3.

[112] Payen, *De Matrimonio,* II, in appendix.

also requires that the *Defensor* sign the despositions of parties, witnesses and experts.[113]

It would hardly seem that the Roman authorities view this requirement as useless. Both of these instructions were issued after the Code. Neither has this particular point in the legislation any particular bearing on the peculiar conditions that these two instructions were intended to cover.

The instruction to China, for the most part seems to be a more detailed explanation of the law intended to help the busy missionary to cope with these problems more effectively despite his many other duties. It does indeed carry several exemptions from the general law of the Church but this is not one of them. The instruction with regard to the investigation that must accompany the request for a dispensation from a nonconsummated marriage certainly has for its purpose to legislate more carefully for this most important investigation. For this reason it is more explicit than the general law, and does depart from it at times due to the special nature of the purpose of the investigation. However the point under discussion is not one of these departures, and it seems at this point merely to give a more detailed version of the common law.

However cogent these arguments may be, doubt still attaches to the obligation of the *Defensor* to sign these depositions.[114] If he wishes to do so, he should sign after the witness and judge have signed in turn, and before the notary whose signature should be last. This is the order prescribed for the signing of depositions by all the official instructions covering this particular phase of the trial.[115]

Article VIII

The *Defensor Vinculi* and the Experts in the Trial

Among those who give testimony during the trial there is one

[113] *Regulae Servandae Super Rato*, n. 46.

[114] Canon 1780, § 2.

[115] S. C. C., Instr., August 22, 1840—*Fontes*, n. 4069; S. C. S. Off., Instr. (*ad Ep. Rituum Orient.*), a. 1883, n. 14—*Fontes*, n. 1076; S. C. de Prop. Fid., *Pro Causis Matrimonialibus, ex indulto in Sinis Servanda*, n. 14—*cf.* Payen, *De Matrimonio*, II, in appendix; *Reg. Serv. Super Rato, S. C. de Sacram.*, May 7, 1923, n. 46—*AAS*, XV (1923), p. 397.

group that forms a special class. These are the experts called to assist the judge by giving the court the benefit of their special knowledge.[116]

These experts may be handwriting experts called in to examine a document and verify a signature,[117] but more frequently in matrimonial cases they are medical specialists called to verify the presence or absence of physical or mental defects in one or both of the parties to the marriage.[118]

These experts are to be selected by the judge, but in doing so he must give the *Defensor* opportunity to take exception to the selection if he sees fit to do so.[119]

There is no need to consider when the services of these experts are required as this does not fall within the scope of this work. Suffice it to say that they are required whenever the judge finds their help necessary, in cases where nullity is based on impotency, and in cases where request is made for a dispensation from a nonconsummated marriage unless there is other proof that would render their services unnecessary.[120] It is well to note that they are required also when defective consent is based on insanity.[121]

It is the duty of the *Defensor* in common with the judge to see to it that the experts meet all the requirements of the law, namely that they are personally qualified to give testimony, that their reputation in their field is merited, and that in the fulfillment of their duties they have observed the regulations laid down by the court to prevent the fraudulent substitution of one person for another.[122]

The *Defensor* also has the general duty in common with the judge to see that all the regulations of the law are carried out as found in

[116] Canon 1792; Payen, *De Matrimonio,* III, n. 2692, 1.

[117] Canon 1800.

[118] Canons 1976, 1982.

[119] Canon 1793, § 2; A Coronata, *De Processibus,* p. 229, n. 1325, II; Payen, *De Matrimonio,* III, n. 2692, 2; S. C. C. Instr., August 22, 1840—*Fontes,* n. 4069.

[120] Canon 1976; Sipos, *Enchiridion,* p. 847.

[121] Canon 1982; Sipos, *Enchiridion,* p. 847.

[122] Canons 1795, 1796 ff.: S. C. de Sacram. Instr., March 27, 1929.

canons 1759 and following, as well as those of Article II, of the First Part of the Fourth Book of the Code.[123]

The experts who examine the spouses in matrimonial trials must be two in number, and after making their examinations individually they are obliged to submit separate reports to the court in writing.[124]

The *Defensor* studies these reports as well as the judge, and then draws up a set of questions with which the judge will examine each expert.[125] These questions must be presented to the court closed and sealed, and should not be opened until the examination is about to begin.[126]

The notary's written record of this examination is then signed by the expert himself, and by the judge. The *Defensor* certainly may sign the deposition if he so wishes, but may not be forced to do so in ordinary cases by the common law.[127]

In the investigation to ascertain the existence of grounds for the dispensation from nonconsummated marriage he is bound by the regulations of the *Regulae Servandae* of the Sacred Congregation of the Sacraments to sign these depositions.[128]

Article IX

The Duties of the *Defensor Vinculi* in Connection with Rogatory Commissions

Every tribunal has the right to call another tribunal to its assistance for the purpose of citing and examining witnesses and documents.[129] This may be found to be necessary when witnesses or the

[123] Benedict XIV, const., *Dei Miseratione,* November 3, 1741, n. 6, " . . . voce et scriptis Matrimonii validatatem tueri . . . "—*Fontes,* n. 318.

[124] Canon 1980, § 2; Wernz-Vidal, *Jus Canonicum,* V, p. 839.

[125] Canon 1981; Sipos, *Enchiridion,* p. 881; Wernz-Vidal, *Jus Canonicum,* V, p. 839; Santi, *Praelectiones J. C.,* lib. IV, p. 157, n. 45.

[126] Canon 1968, 1°; Santi, *Praelectiones J. C.,* lib. IV, p. 157, n. 45; S. C. C., Instr., August 22, 1840, "peracta relatione a singulis seorsim, defensor matrimonii exhibet interrogatoria clausa, sigillata, super quibus fieri debet examen peritorum"—*Fontes,* n. 4069.

[127] Canon 1780, § 2; *cf.* preceding Article.

[128] *Reg. Servandae Super Rato,* n. 46

[129] Canon 1570, § 2.

possessors of documents live in another diocese or in a distant part of the same diocese, and consequently would find it gravely difficult to appear before the tribunal that is trying the case.[180]

Just what is the duty and the obligation of the *Defensor* when this method of examining a witness is resorted to in a case in which he is acting?

His first duty is to prepare the set of questions for the examination of the person to be questioned. These questions closed and sealed, are then dispatched to the Curia which is to execute the rogatory commission.[181]

This is not explicitly contained in the law of the Code, but it is most certainly implicitly contained in canon 1570, § 2, which gives one tribunal the right to the service of another and which reads in part:

> . . . ius habet in auxilium vocandi aliud tribunal, quod normas pro singulis actibus iure praescriptas servare debet.

How does the Holy See interpret this particular canon? It is quite evident that the greater part of the *Regulae Servandae* for the *ratum et non consummatum* process is merely a more explicit statement of the law of the Code. This particular phase of the trial is an instance of this fact. The *Regulae* in legislating for the hearing of witnesses in other dioceses, decrees that the judge should request the Ordinary of the witness to cite him before his own tribunal, and there examine him according to the questions of the *Defensor Vinculi* that were sent to him. It also adds that the Ordinary is then to send the records of the hearing to the judge after the examination has been completed.[182]

This procedure imposed by the instruction of the Sacred Congregation of the Sacraments, is in perfect harmony with the former instruction issued by the Sacred Congregation of the Council in 1840, for the regulation of all matrimonial trials.[183]

[180] Canon 1770, 3°, 2°.

[181] S. C. C. Instr., August 22, 1840—*Fontes,* n. 4069.

[182] *Regulae Servandae Super Rato,* n. 23.

[183] S. C. C., Instr., August 22, 1840—" . . . examinandi juxta interrogatoria ab eodem defensore conficienda . . . "—*Fontes,* n. 4069.

The duty of the *Defensor* to draw up the list of questions to be used by the judge of the assisting tribunal is therefore very clear. The doubt with regard to his duty may arise on this point with regard to a slightly different application of his duty. Should the assisting tribunal call in its own *Defensor* to assist at the examination of the witness?

The Code contains no specific legislation with regard to this point, hence it is necessary to have recourse to the prior law in order to discern the proper interpretation of the present law on this point.

The instruction issued by the Sacred Congregation of the Council in the year 1840[134] does supply a rule to cover this particular phase of the trial. The instruction declares that the questions drawn up by the *Defensor Vinculi* are to be dispatched closed and sealed to the Bishop of the place where the witness now dwells. This Bishop is then to elect a suitable person who is to fulfill the duties of the *Defensor Validitatis Matrimonii* according to the law of Benedict XIV.[135]

The instruction of the Holy Office sent to the Oriental Bishops in the year 1883, and to the Bishops of the United States in the same year by the Sacred Congregation of the Propagation of the Faith, likewise supports this interpretation of the law.[136]

This instruction provides that the questions of the *Defensor* are to be sent to the Ordinary of the place where the witness or witnesses reside with the names of those to be examined, and that he is to examine the witnesses himself, or to delegate his Vicar General or some other qualified priest, receiving the oath from the witnesses and observing all the other prescriptions previously mentioned; "*. . . et caeteris servatis quae supra praescripta sunt.*"

Prominent among these requirements at that time was that which required the *Defensor* to sign the depositions after the witness and judge and before the notary.[137] Evidently he was expected to be present.

[134] *Fontes,* n. 4069.

[135] Benedict XIV, const., *Dei Miseratione,* November 3, 1741—*Fontes* n. 318.

[136] N. 15—*Fontes,* n. 1076.

[137] *Loc. cit.*

It would certainly seem that these instructions call for the active presence of a *Defensor Vinculi* even at these hearings.

It can hardly be claimed that these instructions have been changed on this point by the Code. Section 15 of the instruction sent to China in the year 1929 for the regulation of matrimonial trials there [138] is identical in every respect with section 15 of the instruction of 1883. This section does not embody any exception to the general law of the Church now in force, rather it is more in the nature of an official commentary for the use of those who work in the Mission Field.

Canon 1570 of the Code itself also supports this view for it also maintains that the tribunal in examining a witness for another court should observe all the regulations for the particular acts of the trial; "*. . . quod normas pro singulis actibus iure praescriptas servare debet.*"

It is therefore quite evident from the intrinsic examination of the law, that the tribunal executing the rogatory commission should call in its own *Defensor* to assist at the hearing, and that the *Defensor* when thus present enjoys all the rights that he would have if he were acting in a case pertaining to his own court.

However, since the Code does not specifically demand his presence, and since the questions of the other *Defensor* must be used, the claim of nullity against the *acta* cannot well be maintained. This is especially so in view of canon 15 [139] as well as in view of the fact that the *Defensor* certainly will study the results of these examinations on their return from the other court, and thus the *acta* would be sanated if perchance their validity were endangered through violation of canon 1587, § 1.[140]

However, every indication points to the fact that the *Defensor* of the Curia should be present at these hearings. The mere fact that a witness is to be questioned outside the tribunal should not

[138] *Cf.* Payen, *De Matrimonio*, II, in appendix.

[139] "Leges, etiam irritantes et inhabilitantes, in dubio iuris non urgent . . . "

[140] "Si legitime citati aliquibus actibus non interfuerint, acta quidem valent, verum postea eorum examini subiicienda omnino sunt ut ea omnia sive voce sive scriptis possint animadvertere et proponere quae necessaria aut opportuna iudicaverint"—Canon 1587, § 2.

serve to exempt the act from the regular procedure of the law. In fact greater diligence should be exercised by judge and *Defensor* in these examinations, for they are somewhat handicapped inasmuch as they are unfamiliar with the case.

Article X

The Declaration of Contumacy and Its Reference to the *Defensor Vinculi*

Contumacy in the technical canonical sense is the formal disobedience of the court evinced by one, who having been properly cited, has failed to answer either in person or by means of a procurator. On the verification of the legitimate reception of the citation, and the party's lack of excuse, the judge may declare the party to be contumacious.[141]

Upon the pronouncement of this decree the party who has thus failed to obey the court, falls under certain legal disabilities. If he is the *actor,* in the case, he loses his right to prosecute the action. However, if the *Defensor Vinculi* were acting in such a case on the side of the plaintiff as he might be in any appellate trial, he has the right to make the case his own.[142]

The *Defensor Vinculi* as an official cannot be declared in contempt, but the holder of the office may be punished and forced to act, if negligent in the exercise of his duties.[143]

The party who has thus shown such disregard for the authority of the court is also liable to punishment,[144] and is also liable to judgment for the judicial expenses.[145]

However, this procedure is of comparatively little importance to the *Defensor*. According to modern practice, it is the *Defensor* who appeals in most cases, and hence it will be most unusual for him to

[141] Canon 1842; A Coronata, *De Processibus,* p. 279, n. 1373; Roberti, *De Processibus*, II, nn. 400, 405.

[142] Canon 1850, §§ 1, 2; A Coronata, *De Processibus,* p. 285, n. 1379, 2°.

[143] *Cf.* Canon 1986.

[144] Canon 1845, §§ 1, 2.

[145] Canon 1851, §§ 1, 2.

make his own, the case of an *actor* who has been adjudged in contempt according to canon 1850, § 1.

It would be well for him to keep his right to seek a declaration of contumacy against one of the parties in mind,[146] since he may find this proceeding to be of great advantage to his cause, giving him an easy means of quashing a case in first instance, in which the declaration could be obtained against the *actor*, the one alleging the nullity of the marriage.

Article XI

The Duty of the *Defensor Vinculi* with Regard to Documents Entered in the Trial

The *Defensor* has the duty to inspect all documents entered as proofs in the trial, especially when they militate against the validity of the marriage in question before the court.[147]

This implies that he must ascertain that the document is truly genuine and that it is properly valuated. He should also make certain that the document really applies to the case before the court. According to his general mandate he of course when necessary may attack the documents as forgeries, or attack the signatures, or strive to forestall any other attempt to perpetrate fraud on the court.[148]

It is possible, too, that a document desired as a proof by one of the parties may be in the possession of the other party. In this case the party desiring the court to see the document, petitions the judge giving a description of the document, and the reason for the petition, indicating also the possessor. If the other party denies that he has the document, or refuses to present it to the court, the judge after hearing the *Defensor Vinculi*, may by interlocutory sentence order the holder to bring it into the court.

It will be noticed that the *Defensor* must be heard before the judge issues this decree or interlocutory sentence. It is well to

[146] Canon 1844, §1; A Coronata, *De Processibus*, p. 282, n. 1376, 3°; Roberti, *De Processibus*, II, n. 405.

[147] Canon 1969, 2°.

[148] Canon 1969, 4°.

note that the *Defensor* also has the right to petition for the exhibition of a document in this manner which may be in the possession of one of the parties opposing him.[149]

Article XII

The *Defensor Vinculi* and the Suppletory Oath

The *Defensor* may also petition the judge to administer the suppletory oath to one of the parties.[150] This is an oath which the judge may administer to one of the parties to the trial for the purpose of strengthening or completing the proofs presented to the court.[151]

The oath may be administered by the judge on his own initiative, or at the instance of one of the parties as well as at the request of the *Defensor Vinculi.*[152]

The *Defensor* may find it occasionally useful to demand that the oath be administered to quash an incomplete attack on the validity of a marriage, as would be the case when he uses this oath to render complete the arguments on the side of validity. On the whole, however, the oath will be of little importance to him, for it is incapable of rendering an incomplete case against the validity of the marriage complete or conclusive.

The suppletory oath cannot be used to complete a judicial argument that will serve to decide a matter of grave importance,[153] and the validity of a marriage, a sacrament is certainly a matter of supreme importance. It is equally certain that proofs that need the support of the suppletory oath cannot upset the presumption of validity that marriage enjoys before the law.[154]

149 Canons 1824, § 1; 1969, 4°; Roberti, *De Processibus,* II, n. 375.

150 Canon 1830, § 3.

151 Canon 1829; *Regulae S. R. Rotae,* n. 155, 1°; Wernz-Vidal, *Jus Canonicum,* VI, n. 528.

152 Canon 1830, § 3; Roberti, *De Processibus,* II, n. 384; A Coronata, *De Processibus,* p. 266, n. 1361; Sipos, *Enchiridion,* p. 851.

153 Canon 1830, § 2; Roberti, *De Processibus,* II, p. 111, n. 381.

154 Canon 1014; Vermeersch-Creusen, *Epitome,* II, n. 279; Gasparri, *De Matrimonio* (edit. 1932), II, p. 300, n. 1275.

Hence, while it may be useful for the *Defensor* to use the right to request the administration of the oath on rare occasion, it will never become a matter of great importance to him in the exercise of his duties.

Article XIII

The Duty of the *Defensor Vinculi* in Reference to the Interpreters

When the service of an interpreter is found to be necessary in a trial, the interpreter of course by express provision of the Code, must be designated by the judge and sworn in before being permitted to function before the court. The interpreter must be acceptable to the parties and also to the *Defensor Vinculi.* He must be sufficiently proficient in the required language and must not be liable to the charge of prejudice which may be made by either the parties or the *Defensor Vinculi.*[155]

In this connection it will be noticed that the *Defensor* has the right to take exception to the interpreter, if he finds it necessary to do so to protect the ends of justice. The *Defensor* has the right to be present at all the sessions of the trial and consequently has the right to be present at the selection of an interpreter,[156] since being present he is bound to do everything in his power legitimately to protect the validity of the sacrament that is being attacked.[157]

This means that the *Defensor* is bound in conscience to assure himself that the interpreter is capable, and not otherwise legitimately impeded from performing his duties before the court.

Article XIV

The *Defensor Vinculi* and Ocular Inspection (*Accessus Judicialis*)

In the course of a trial, the judge may find it necessary under certain circumstances to go to a place, locality or house figuring

[155] Canon 1614; Roberti, *De Processibus,* I, n. 126.

[156] Canon 1969, 1°.

[157] Canon 1968, 3°.

prominently in the case, in order that he may better understand and evaluate the arguments adduced by the parties.[158] While this necessity will arise but seldom, yet it may occur at any time. Perhaps the credibility of an important witness may hinge upon whether it is humanly possible to see or hear in one place what occurred in another place nearby. Suppose at the same time that the testimony of the other witnesses was in disagreement. This would indeed be an instance in which the judge could well make an ocular inspection, go himself, and examine the ground and then determine the relative value of the testimony that he has heard.

In a marriage case the judge may act on his own initiative,[159] but the *Defensor,* too, could demand that this procedure be used, and could only be denied his petition by unanimous decision on the part of the three judges.[160]

He, too, would have the right to accompany the judge and notary on their visit for this is a judicial act and consequently he is privileged to be present.[161]

If there is any doubt that this is a part of the trial, a truly judicial act, it will be quickly dispelled when it is realized that the judge can hear witnesses when making this official visit.[162] Since this is possible, then the *Defensor* has a right to be present by virtue of canon 1968, 1°.

The *Defensor* negatively could also raise objections against this proceeding, if for instance he had good reason to believe that conditions were changed for the purpose of deceiving the judge. This he may do by virtue of the general duty imposed on him by the third section of canon 1968.[163]

[158] Canon 1806; Roberti, *De Processibus,* II, n. 364.

[159] Canon 1618.

[160] Canon 1969, 4°; Roberti, *De Processibus,* II, n. 365.

[161] Canon 1587, § 2.

[162] Canon 1810.

[163] " . . . eaque omnia deducere, quae ad matrimonium tuendum utilia censuerit."

Article XV

Two Minor Applications of the Rights of the *Defensor Vinculi* to the Law of the Trial

The judge either immediately before or during a trial is empowered to order a document or other object of value to be placed in the custody of a third party to safeguard the rights of the one seeking such protection.[164]

If this safeguard is sought before the opening of the trial it is handled like any other question that involves the right of action before the court. If it occurs during the trial itself it is handled after the fashion of an incidental cause.[165]

In matrimonial trials as in other cases involving the common good, the judge may order this precaution to be taken on his own initiative as often as the need arises.[166]

In addition, both *Defensor Vinculi* and the parties have the right to petition this same form of relief from the judge when they fear that the destruction of a document or other instrument will gravely impair their case.[167]

The *Defensor* can in like manner [168] obtain from the judge a decree prohibiting the exercise of rights that would tend to prejudice and hurt his case for validity.

While these rights will not be of great utility to the *Defensor* under ordinary circumstances, they may well repay him on occasion for a knowledge of them.

In connection with sequestration, it will be well to note that it is given to protect material goods movable or immovable. The one seeking the protection of this safeguard of the law is not obliged to fully vindicate his or her right to the object, inasmuch as the decree of sequestration may be issued to protect a conditional or a disputed right. Hence, it is only necessary to prove the probability of

[164] Canon 1672, § 1.

[165] Roberti, *De Processibus,* I, n. 232, 2°.

[166] Canon 1672, § 3; Sipos, *Enchiridion,* p. 828.

[167] Canon 1672, §§ 1, 3.

[168] Canon 1672, § 2.

both the danger, and the right.[169] The petitioner should also demonstrate that he is threatened with a loss or a danger that cannot well be remedied or forestalled in any other fashion. In other words he must indicate that there is no other means open to him that will protect his rights without grave inconvenience. The reason is, that sequestration is an extraordinary legal precaution, and should not be used where another would suffice.[170]

The *Defensor Vinculi* finding it necessary to obtain a judicial decree prohibiting the exercise of rights, will act in the same manner that he would in seeking the sequestration of an object or document.[171]

The case is not inconceivable in which under this action he would seek to have the parties separated. He might have many reasons for such action. He is not officially concerned with the danger of sin, but he might fear the corrupting influence of an unprincipled spouse over the other party to the marriage, who for instance might seek to persuade the other party to commit perjury, and thus injure the case for validity and result in a sentence for nullity at variance with truth.[172]

169 Roberti, *De Processibus,* I, n. 232.

170 Canon 1674; Roberti, *De Processibus,* I, n. 232, c.

171 Canon 1672, § 2; Roberti, *De Processibus,* I, n. 233.

172 *Cf.* Roberti, *De Processibus,* I, n. 233.

CHAPTER IV

THE *DEFENSOR VINCULI* IN THE REMAINING STAGES OF THE TRIAL

ARTICLE I

THE *Conclusio in Causa* AND *Publicatio Processus*

THE first part of the trial is devoted to the hearing of witnesses and experts, in a word to the gathering of evidence. It is concerned only with the facts in the case. When all the facts pertinent to the case have been gathered, the trial enters the second major phase wherein the opposing advocates take the facts and explain them in the light of the law.[1]

These two stages of the trial are divided by the *conclusio in causa,*[2] which is decreed by the judge. Once this decree has been issued the entire nature of the process has been changed. The court's primary concern now is the application of the law to the facts brought to the attention of the court in the earlier sessions of the trial.[3]

The judge may issue the decree closing the process only after the *Defensor Vinculi* and the parties have intimated that they have nothing further to bring before the court. The judge may also decree the *conclusio in causa* if it is evident that one or both of the parties are calling witnesses merely to delay the trial or confuse the issue, or if the court feels that it is sufficiently instructed.[4]

Since the next step in the trial is the discussion of the case in which both sides apply the law to the facts in the case, and since all the testimony has been kept secret by the court, the judge must issue another decree, that of the publication of the testimony by

[1] Roberti, *De Processibus,* II, n. 434.

[2] Canon 1860, § 1.

[3] Roberti, *De Processibus,* II, n. 434.

[4] Canon 1860, §§ 2, 3; Roberti, *De Processibus,* II, n. 437, b.

which the opposing parties are given the right to acquaint themselves with all the evidence collected by the court.[5]

It is quite impossible to consider the effects of the *publicatio processus* without considering also the effects of the *conclusio in causa.* These two decrees are intimately connected. It is possible to theorize upon the order in which the two decrees should be issued, but the question is devoid of practical value. The two decrees divide the trial into two parts and belong to neither. Before proceeding further it will be necessary to pause and consider these two decrees a little more thoroughly in the light of the rights and duties of the *Defensor Vinculi.*

The judge must first have obtained the admission from the *Defensor Vinculi* that he has rested his case, before proceeding to the issuance of the decree closing the process. The *Defensor* must either indicate that he has nothing further to say or fail to make use of a period set aside for the production of witnesses or other evidence. The *Defensor* is not given this right explicitly in the Code itself. It does explicitly give the right to the parties in the case. *A pari,* the *Defensor* should also enjoy this right.[6] Additional support is given to this conclusion by the Pre-Code law, inasmuch as the *Defensor Vinculi* was obliged to sign the decree closing the cause, after the judge and before the notary.[7]

After the issuance of this decree new evidence is not to be introduced as a general rule,[8] inasmuch as both parties and *Defensor* have indicated that they have no further evidence to bring to the attention of the court.[9] New evidence ordinarily may not be heard after the *publicatio processus* except under certain circumstances fixed by law.[10]

[5] Canons 1858, 1859; Roberti, *De Processibus,* II, n. 435.

[6] Canon 1860, § 2; Payen, *De Matrimonio,* III, n. 2702, 3; Wernz-Vidal, *Jus Canonicum,* V, n. 702.

[7] S. C. C. Instr., August 22, 1840—" . . . factis subscriptionibus ab eo [iudice] a defensore matrimonii, et a cancellario"—*Fontes,* n. 4069; S. C. S. Off., Instr. (*ad Ep. Rituum Orient.*), a. 1883, Tit., III, n. 22—*Fontes,* n. 1076.

[8] Canon 1861, § 1; Roberti, *De Processibus,* II, n. 438.

[9] Canon 1860, § 2; Roberti, *De Processibus,* II, n. 437.

[10] Canon 1786.

The *Defensor Vinculi* on the contrary is not so strictly bound by these restrictions, nor does he need the grave reason required by canon 1786 for the introduction of new evidence or witnesses.[11] He is obliged none the less to make sure that no danger of fraud exists, not by canon 1786 but by the general demands of justice and of his office.

The *conclusio in causa* therefore has but little effect on the rights of the *Defensor Vinculi,* except to impose on him the duty of caution lest in calling a witness after the testimony has been published he should give him the opportunity to deceive the court.

The *Defensor Vinculi* still retains the right to object to the calling of a witness by one of the parties after the *conclusio in causa,* when he fears that the danger of fraud or collusion has not been removed.[12]

The *Defensor Vinculi* himself, in seeking to call a witness at any time in the trial, may be refused only by unanimous decision of the judges.[13]

The exercise of these or any right of the *Defensor Vinculi* should be properly credited to him in the *acta,* the minutes of the trial, in order that the superior tribunal may not be improperly influenced or misled.[14]

Article II

The Summing Up (*Discussio Causae*)

The *conclusio causae* does not pertain to the first phase of the trial. It serves to divide this first part devoted solely to the securing of evidence from the second phase of the trial which is devoted to the application of the law to the facts in the case.

Once the case has been closed the second or forensic stage of the trial begins. All the facts in the case have been gathered, the opposing advocates now explain them in the light of the law.[15]

[11] Canon 1969, 3°.

[12] Canons 1983, §§ 1, 2; 1786; A Coronata, *De Processibus,* p. 220, n. 1312, 2°, p. 432, n. 1495.

[13] Canon 1969, 4°.

[14] A Coronata, *De Processibus,* p. 421, n. 1484.

[15] Roberti, *De Processibus,* II, n. 434; Sipos, *Enchiridion,* p. 881.

The *Defensor Vinculi* is most active in this stage of the trial, for he is explicitly bound in virtue of his office to produce arguments for validity and against the nullity of the marriage.[16]

During the period of time fixed by the judge, the advocates write their defenses or arguments, making a copy for each judge, the *Defensor Vinculi* and the other party or parties.[17] After the arguments have been interchanged by the parties they then write their respective answers. They have the right to answer only once unless the judge extends the right by decree.[18]

To what extent is the *Defensor Vinculi* bound by these regulations? To take an active part in this discussion he is certainly bound. He is strictly bound by virtue of his office to submit arguments against nullity and in support of the validity of the marriage.[19] The *Defensor* too, should submit these arguments in writing, since he cannot claim any exemption from this requirement inasmuch as he is bound to defend the validity of the marriage in writing as well as orally.[20]

The duty of restraining and regulating the conduct of this phase of the trial, of course, pertains to the judge. The *Defensor* should maintain the effectiveness of his arguments, drawing them up as concisely and forcefully as possible.[21]

The parties should write their arguments first, and copies should be given to the *Defensor Vinculi* who then should write his own argument. Frequently, however, the *Defensor* will be the only defendant in the case but even in this case he is not obliged to write his argument until after he receives that of the plaintiff.

The answers are written in the same order, but the *Defensor* will always enjoy the right to answer last. Copies of all arguments and answers should be supplied to the judges, the *Defensor Vinculi*, the other party, and to the notary. The *Defensor*, therefore, should

16 Canon 1968, 3°; Roberti, *De Processibus*, II, n. 439; Wernz-Vidal, *Jus Canonicum*, VI, n. 584; Mansella, *De Impedimentis*, p. 210.

17 Canon 1863, §§ 1, 2.

18 Canon 1865, §§ 1, 2.

19 Canon 1968, 3°; Roberti, *De Processibus*, II, n. 439; A Coronata, *De Processibus*, p. 298, n. 1389, III; Wernz-Vidal, *Jus Canonicum*, VI, n. 584.

20 Canons 1863, § 1; 1968, 3°.

21 Roberti, *De Processibus*, II, p. 163, n. 440.

supply copies of his arguments and answers to the judges, the parties and the notary.[22]

The proper procedure for the interchange of these arguments is to despatch them to the Curia, which then in turn sends them to the proper persons or officials. Many Curias, however, have developed a practice of their own in this matter, regulated either by formally adopted statutes or simply defined by custom.

In general the plaintiff always speaks first, then the defendant followed by the Promotor of Justice if he is in the case, and finally the *Defensor Vinculi*. The *Defensor* always speaks last.[23]

The *Defensor Vinculi* may find himself in a case where he is alone in the defense of validity, both parties either seeking nullity, or the one being in default. In this case, the *Defensor Vinculi* will be bound by the necessities of the occasion to speak in the second place in response to the claims of the plaintiff. This in no ways offers any contradiction or opposition to his right to speak last. He still retains that right, regardless of the fact that he has spoken in answer to the plaintiff. He was forced to do this by the exigencies of the occasion, for if he should fail to do so, the hearing would not develop properly. It is possible but not usual for the Promotor of Justice to be active in a marriage case in urging the nullity of the marriage. In the event that he is active, the *actor* or plaintiff, would speak first, then the *Defensor Vinculi* as defendant, finally the Promotor of Justice, followed by the *Defensor*, who may speak again by virtue of the right explicitly given to him in canon 1984, § 1. The judge cannot proceed to the final sentence, unless the *Defensor Vinculi* first declare that he has rested his case.[24]

It must be borne in mind that the *Defensor Vinculi* does not write his defense or argument simultaneously with the plaintiff or the defendant. He first receives their arguments, and then proceeds to write his own.[25]

[22] Canon 1863, §§ 1, 2; Roberti, *De Processibus,* p. 164, n. 440.

[23] Canon 1984, § 1; A Coronata, *De Processibus,* p. 300, n. 1391; Muñiz, *Procedimientos Eccles.,* III, p. 427.

[24] Canon 1984, § 2.

[25] Canon 1968, 3°; S. C. S. Off. Instr. (*ad Ep. Rituum Orient.*), a. 1883, Tit. III, n. 23—" . . . communicandae erunt defensori vinculi Matrimonialis, ut

Therefore if both the plantiff and the defendant are active in the case, both of their summations go to the *Defensor Vinculi.* If not, he receives the argument of the plaintiff and proceeds to write his own argument.

A Coronata in his work *De Processibus* states that the Promotor of Justice and the *Defensor Vinculi* are not bound by the time limits set by the judge for the writing of these defenses, unless they are sustaining the roles of parties in the case.[26] This is quite true, but it is not as absolute with regard to the *Defensor Vinculi* as it might seem at first sight.

If the *Defensor Vinculi* is sustaining the role of the defendant in a case, he is forced to answer the plaintiff within the time set by the judge in order to insure the proper progress of the trial. As pointed out above, this fact does not deprive the *Defensor* of any of his rights, mainly that of answering last, as this is secured for him in the Code in the most explicit fashion.[27] The *Defensor* should not be regarded as wishing unnecessarily to delay the trial, for in doing so he would be acting against the demands of strict justice. The parties before the court have a right to a prompt decision, not out of charity but out of justice, hence unreasonably to deprive them of their right is to violate that precept. Regardless of whether the *Defensor Vinculi* is bound to observe the time limits set by the judge, he always has the right to present new arguments at any time in the trial before the final sentence.[28]

Therefore in one sense the *Defensor Vinculi* can never be absolutely bound by these limits set by the judge in virtue of canon 1865, § 1, § 2, since he may only be denied the right to present new arguments or proofs by unanimous decision of the judges.[29] The judges cannot in conscience refuse the *Defensor Vinculi* if they feel that he may bring forth matter relevant to the trial, since a decision

eas expendere, et quatenus Matrimonii validitatem impugnent, refutare, valeat" —*Fontes,* n. 1076; Roberti, *De Processibus,* II, p. 165, n. 440, 2.

[26] A Coronata, *De Processibus,* p. 299, n. 1390.

[27] Canon 1984, § 1—"Defensor vinculi jus habet ut in allegando, petendo et respondendo tam in scriptis quam in defensione orali, audiatur postremus."

[28] Canon 1969, 3°.

[29] Canon 1969, 4°.

in these trials if at variance with the objective truth may be the cause of sin. Of course failure to utilize a period fixed by the judge for the production of further argument, may be interpreted as equivalent to a statement by the *Defensor* that he rests his case. This, however, takes place at the close of deliberative sessions of the trial, and failure by the *Defensor* to take advantage of this period permits the judge to proceed to the giving of the final sentence.[30] If the spouses are active in the trial as plaintiff and defendant, the *Defensor* will not be obliged to observe the time limits set by the judge.[31]

This exemption will not be of any great advantage to the *Defensor Vinculi* in the general run of cases since he is bound by his office to take an active part in the discussion of the case,[32] and he will only be delaying the trial without reason if he withholds his arguments. If he submits them at the end of the exchange by the parties, the trial will have to be further delayed to give them the opportunity to answer his arguments. It would further the expediting of the trial, if after the written defenses of the parties reach him, he were to write his own argument, and thus enable them to answer both their own arguments and his as well. Then when the replies of the parties reach the *Defensor Vinculi,* he will be enabled to answer all objections that may have arisen against his arguments.

In these sessions the parties normally will be permitted but one reply, which should be made in writing. Copies of these replies should be furnished to the opposing party, the *Defensor Vinculi* and the judges in the usual manner.[33]

The judge may also permit a brief oral discussion of the case, at the instance of the *Defensor Vinculi* or of one or both of the parties.[34]

When this procedure is permitted the parties may submit statements of the facts which the discussion is to cover. Generally how-

[30] Canon 1984, § 3, "Si vero ante praefinitum a judice iudicii diem, defensor nihil deduxerit, praesumitur eum nihil iam deducendum habere."

[31] Canon 1862, § 1; A Coronata, *De Processibus,* p. 99, n. 1390.

[32] Canon 1968, 3°; A Coronata, *De Processibus,* p. 298, n. 1389, III; Roberti, *De Processibus,* II, n. 439.

[33] Canon 1865, §§ 1, 2; Roberti, *De Processibus,* II, p. 165, n. 440, 2.

[34] Canon 1866, § 2.

ever, the oral discussion will assume the form of questions and answers. The *Defensor* will enjoy the similar right to submit statements or questions for use in the discussion.[35]

The *Defensor Vinculi* has the strict right and duty to be present at this oral discussion, and he should be cited to attend it, inasmuch as it is truly a part of the trial.[36]

In connection with this phase of the trial, and with the whole trial it must be remembered that the *Defensor* always enjoys the right to seek extensions of time for the purpose of writing additional arguments,[37] and may be refused only by unanimous decision of the judges.[38]

The *Defensor Vinculi* also enjoys the right to answer last in any discussion during the trial, regardless of whether the discussion is oral or written.[39]

The practical result of this right is seen in the requirement that the judge cannot proceed to the declaration of the final sentence, unless the *Defensor* first have intimated that he has rested his case.

This right to speak last, should not be understood in such a way as to give the *Defensor Vinculi* the right to obstruct the progress of the trial arbitrarily. The right of the parties to services and the decision of the tribunal is a right belonging to them in strict justice, and hence, merely obstructive tactics on the part of the *Defensor Vinculi* would not only bring no benefit to his case, but would be unjust in the strict sense. The judges are fully empowered to overrule actions and pleas unsupported by reason, and in event of their exercise he may impose punishments and damages on the guilty person, the *Defensor Vinculi* not excluded.[40]

Article III

The *Defensor Vinculi* and the Final Sentence

The definitive sentence of the court should be pronounced as soon

[35] Canons 1968, 3°; 1969, 4°.

[36] Canons 1587, §§ 1, 2; 1968, 3°.

[37] Canon 1969, 1°.

[38] Canon 1969, 4°.

[39] Canon 1984, § 1; A Coronata, *De Processibus*, p. 432, n. 1496.

[40] Canons 1864, 1625, §§ 1, 2, 3.

as possible after the termination of the discussion of the case or the summing up. The judge, if necessary, may fix a time for judicial study of the case before the sentence is drawn up.[41]

The sentence is the legal pronouncement by which the tribunal defines the question proposed by the litigants, and examined by the court.[42]

Since at least three judges must try all solemn matrimonial cases in which the bond of marriage is involved,[43] it is necessary for these judges to meet in order to formulate the collegiate sentence. The conduct of this meeting and the actual evolution of the sentence, are strictly regulated by the law.

On the day appointed the judges meet, each bringing with him his written opinion. They then compare their opinions, in order to arrive at the opinion which will be that of the collegiate tribunal. This the final opinion, which meets the approval of the greater number of the judges, is formally drawn up by the judge selected as the *ponens,* and is signed by all the judges including the dissenting member or members.[44]

Has the *Defensor Vinculi* a right to be present at this meeting? If he has a right, it must be remembered he will also have an obligation to be present. It is generally conceded that the *Defensor Vinculi* has neither right nor duty to be present at this meeting of the judges for the purpose of arriving at their sentence.[45]

The right and the duty of the *Defensor* to presence extends only to the judicial sessions of the trial. The discussion of the judges for the formation of the sentence is not judicially a part of the trial. This is shown by the absence of the notary.[46] This meeting is merely a private gathering of the judges, and the *Defensor* has no more right to be present, than he would have to assist the judge in forming his sentence, if one judge were permitted to hear marriage cases in which the nullity of the sacrament was at stake.

[41] Canon 1870; Wernz-Vidal, *Jus Canonicum,* VI, n. 594.

[42] Canon 1868, § 1; Roberti, *De Processibus,* II, n. 443.

[43] Canons 1576, § 1; 1577, § 1.

[44] Canon 1871, §§ 1-5 incl.

[45] Roberti, *De Processibus,* II, n. 455; A Coronata, *De Processibus,* p. 310, n. 1400; *Regulae S. R. Rotae,* n. 177.

[46] *Cf.* canon 1871.

The absence of the notary is a strong evidence of the nonjudicial character of the meeting, his place being filled by the *ponens*.[47] Additional strength is given to the view by the secrecy with which the law circumscribes the minority opinion of the judges who actually dissent from the collegiate sentence.[48]

It is at best extremely doubtful that this is a judicial proceeding, and therefore the *Defensor Vinculi* has at best an extremely doubtful right to be present. His corresponding obligation to be present is likewise doubtful, and consequently no obligation at all.

The *ponens* who keeps the minutes of this meeting of the judges, draws up the sentence, which must mention the *Defensor Vinculi* if it terminates a trial in which he has intervened.[49]

Article IV

The *Defensor Vinculi* in the Incidental Trial

An incidental trial (*causa incidens*) is a minor trial that occurs during the principal trial. It has for its purpose the settling of a point involved along with the principal claim. This secondary question must be at least implicitly included in the petition by which the plaintiff brought the principal question before the court. It must also be of such a nature, that it must be settled before the main issue can be decided. These secondary questions may be urged at any time during the major trial, from the time of the issuance of the citation by the judge up to the time of the pronouncement of the final sentence.[50]

The incidental cause, a true trial though a secondary one, must be opened by a petition seeking the services of the court in solving the doubt. This petition may be written or oral as the judge sees fit.[51]

[47] Canons 1584, 1871, § 3; 1873, § 2; Roberti, *De Processibus,* II, p. 182.

[48] Canon 1871, § 2; Roberti, *De Processibus,* p. 182; *Regulae S. R. Rotae,* 178, n. 5.

[49] Canon 1874, § 2; A Coronata, *De Processibus,* p. 314, n. 1404, b.

[50] Canon 1837; Roberti, *De Processibus,* II, n. 394; A Coronata, *De Processibus,* p .66, n. 1156, 6°; p. 275, n. 1369; Sipos, *Enchiridion,* p. 851.

[51] Canon 1838; Roberti, *De Processibus,* II, n. 396.

The incidental question may be raised not only at the instance of the parties but also on the motion of the *Defensor Vinculi.*[52]

Being thus able to urge an incidental question before the court, certain special applications of the duties of the *Defensor Vinculi* in this connection present themselves for consideration.

The general rule that is found in canon 1838 first claims attention. This canon states that the regulations of canons 1706 to 1725 are to be applied to the incidental trial in so far as they are feasible.

The incidental trial is opened by the presentation of the petition raising the incidental question to the court. The judge then must decide whether to accept or reject the petition. The judge can make this decision only after having heard the parties and the *Defensor Vinculi.* If the *Defensor* has introduced the petition himself, he may have to defend the introduction of the petition, with regard to its necessity, and connection with the principal question. In opposition to the introduction of an incidental case the *Defensor Vinculi* will be obliged to oppose the acceptance of the petition on the lack of these grounds.[53]

The *Defensor Vinculi,* while obliged to oppose the action if he feels that it is unwarranted in law, has no obligation to oppose it merely because it was introduced by the party contending for the nullity of the marriage. His office never obliges him merely to obstruct the progress of the trial.

In general the same duties devolve on the *Defensor Vinculi* as those which are imposed on him in the principal trial. He is bound to be present at these sessions by the same law that binds him to be present at the sessions of the main trial, for though this is a secondary trial, it is nevertheless a part of the principal trial.

The rules embodied in canons 1706 to 1725 of course cannot be fully applied to these trials because of their nature, and the necessity to facilitate them in order to protect the trial as a whole from undue delay. In essentials they are the same.

The *Defensor Vinculi* is certainly bound to be present at the presentation of the *incidental libellus,* for it is a juridical part of the main trial. The same principle holds true for all the sessions of the

[52] Canon 1837; Roberti, *De Processibus,* II, p. 121, n. 394.

[53] Canon 1839.

incidental trial. True the *Defensor Vinculi* cannot be certainly bound to presence at the presentation of the *libellus* that opens the principal trial, but this is for another reason, namely that the case is not yet before the court as a judicial issue. Here however, a case demanding the presence of the *Defensor Vinculi* is before the court, and he is certainly bound to be present according to the regulations of the law.[54]

Being present therefore at this session, he is obliged to oppose the introduction of the incidental question if it will militate against the discernment of the truth in the case before the court. If it is helpful he is equally bound to support the introduction of the *libellus,* and to seek to insure its acceptance.

If for instance he finds that the question has no essential connection with the main issue and is being agitated only to delay the trial, he is bound by his office to urge the rejection of the incidental petition.

Against the decree of the judge rejecting the incidental question it would seem that the parties and the *Defensor Vinculi* enjoy the use of the same remedy they have at their disposal against the rejection of the principal *libellus.* Canon 1838 applies all the rules *mutatis mutandis* of canons 1706 to 1725 to the conduct of the incidental trial. Canon 1709 gives the right of recourse to the higher tribunal against the rejection of the *libellus.* This right must be exercised within ten days (*tempus utile*) and its exercise should be intimated to the court. The higher court in hearing the recourse would of course have to call in its own *Defensor Vinculi.*[55]

Before leaving this point the writer wishes to observe that canon 1880, 6° does not prohibit the exercise of this recourse. In the first place this is recourse and not appeal, and in the second place the prohibition of the canon refers to appeal from the sentence or decree deciding an incidental question.

If the *Defensor Vinculi* was not permitted to interpose his recourse against the rejection of the incidental *libellus,* he could attack this decree when making his appeal from the final sentence.

If the action of the auditor or judge in refusing the admission

[54] Canons 1586, 1587, 1839.

[55] Canon 1709, § 3.

of the incidental *libellus*, was manifestly unjust, the *Defensor Vinculi* under these conditions may have recourse to the Ordinary.[56]

Against a sentence or decree closing an incidental trial there is no appeal if it lacks definitive effect.[57]

If the interlocutory or incidental sentence does enjoy definitive effect, that is if it estops the principal action then an appeal may be interposed within the regular ten-day period.

Reasoning *a pari* [58] from this principle it might readily be admitted that recourse could be refused against the rejection of the *libellus* of an incidental question which is also lacking in definitive effect. However, authors do not discuss this application of the law, and the question cannot be settled definitely.

If on the other hand the *Defensor* were to agitate the incidental question it would seem that he could be refused only by unanimous decision of the judges.[59]

Whenever the decree closing the incidental question is of such import that it terminates the principal trial, then an appeal may be interposed in the regular way. This would occur in a case where the incidental sentence or decree would relieve the plaintiff of the burden of further proof, or would necessarily force the decision of the judges.[60]

It is well to note that the judge may handle these incidental trials in two ways, either observing all the forms of the regular trial, or by decree following only the essentials of the juridical form.[61]

The *Defensor Vinculi* in this trial enjoys all the rights that he has in the main trial, the right to call witnesses, to have them requestioned, being bound at the same time to supply the questions for the interrogations, and arguments in support of his position in the case. He has the same right to see the *acta* at any time, and to inspect and examine all documents offered as evidence in the case.[62]

[56] Canon 1625, §§ 1, 3.

[57] Canon 1880, 6°.

[58] Canon 20.

[59] Canon 1969, 4°.

[60] Connolly, *Appeals*, p. 81; Reiffenstuel, lib. II, Tit. xxvii, n. 18; Wernz-Vidal, *Jus Canonicum*, VI, n. 606, note 61; Roberti, *De Processibus*, II, n. 446.

[61] Canon 1840, §§ 1, 2, 3.

[62] Canons 1968, 1969, 1838, 1840, 2.

Consequently the *Defensor Vinculi* has the right to be heard last in the incidental trial which he enjoys in the trying of the main issue. The grant of the right to be heard last in canon 1984 is couched in general language, and the incidental trial is not an exception to the general rule, but most conform to the general law of trials in so far as possible.[63]

The *Defensor Vinculi* is therefore, certainly not excluded from participation in the incidental trial. On the contrary, the Code in legislating for these secondary trials, expressly provides for his presence at these proceedings by providing legislation to regulate his actions.[64]

Since the *Defensor Vinculi* never intervenes in a trial except in virtue of strict obligation,[65] it will logically follow that the absence of the *Defensor* from an incidental trial demanding his presence, will nullify the incidental proceedings according to the rule of canon 1587, §§ 1, 2. The incidental trial is merely a part of the principal trial, therefore, if the presence of the *Defensor Vinculi* is required at the one, it will also be required at the other.

The *Defensor Vinculi* will always have been cited with regard to these actions, for he will always have received citation for the trial of the main issue, the nullity or validity of the marriage. Hence if at a later period in the trial he accepts the findings of the tribunal arising out of the incidental hearing, the charge of nullity based on his absence from the incidental trial, could hardly be sustained.[66]

An action to set aside an incidental decree or interlocutory sentence may be entertained at any time during the principal trial previous to the final sentence. In the same manner a partial revision of the incidental sentence may be sought. The action may be taken either at the instance of the judge himself, the parties or the *Defensor Vinculi*. If the action was sought by one of the parties, the judge may grant the request only after first hearing the *Defensor*

[63] "Defensor vinculi ius habet ut in allegando, petendo, et respondendo tam in scriptis quam in defensione orali, audiatur postremus"—Canon 1984, § 1; *cf.* canon 1838.

[64] *Cf.* canons 1837, 1839, 1841.

[65] Canon 1587, § 1.

[66] *Cf.* canon 1587, § 2.

Vinculi and the other party. In the event that the judge wishes to correct or set aside the sentence himself, he must also first have consulted with the *Defensor Vinculi.* In all cases when the motion has not been made by the *Defensor Vinculi* his opinion must have been heard by the court, before the incidental sentence may be corrected or set aside.[67]

In closing it may be said that, while the *Defensor Vinculi* does not enjoy the right to seek to have the incidental decision set aside or corrected by virtue of explicit mention in canon 1841, he is empowered to do so by his general grant of power in canon 1968, 3°.[68]

[67] Canon 1841; A Coronata, *De Processibus,* p. 279, n. 1373, 3°.

[68] " . . . eaque omnia deducere, quae ad matrimonium tuendum utilia censuerit."

CHAPTER V

THE *DEFENSOR VINCULI* IN APPEAL

ARTICLE I

DEFINITIONS

SINCE the Catholic Church is a perfect society,[1] endowed with all the rights and powers necessary for the attainment of its purpose, it necessarily enjoys a threefold power, legislative, executive and judicial. The tribunals through which the Church exercises its judicial power, are divided into three grades. The threefold division begins with the court of the local Bishop as the court of first instance, and continues with that of the Metropolitan, or of another legally chosen Ordinary as the court of second instance. Under the common law of the Church, the court of third instance is always at Rome. The Rota usually hears the cases directed to the Holy See.[2]

The act of appeal is the juridical means by which a question is brought from a lower to a higher court. The act itself is essentially one of the juridical remedies against a definitive sentence. These remedies are three in number, two ordinary remedies, one an extraordinary remedy.

The right of appeal is the ordinary remedy against an unjust sentence, and the complaint of nullity (*querela nullitatis*) the ordinary remedy against an invalid sentence. The extarordinary remedy is the *restitutio in integrum,* a petition to set aside the status of *res iudicata,* which has resulted from the failure to use the right to appeal within the time fixed by law.[3]

The latter remedy, will be of no use to the *Defensor Vinculi.* It is a remedy against a definitive sentence in a case that has become *res iudicata,* and since marriage cases of nullity never attain the status of *res iudicata* [4] this remedy will never serve the *Defensor Vinculi* as a means of furthering his case.

[1] Cappello, *Summa Iuris Publici Ecclesiastici,* p. 139 ff.

[2] Canons 1572, 1594, 1597, 1598.

[3] Canon 1905; Wernz-Vidal, *Jus Canonicum,* VI, n. 600.

[4] Canons 1903, 1989.

The *Defensor Vinculi,* however, will frequently find himself bound to use the two ordinary remedies against the definitive sentence in the ordinary exercise of his duties. These two remedies, that of appeal and of the complaint of nullity are somewhat akin though distinguished by essential differences.

The act of appeal, is an act by which one seeks the aid of a higher tribunal against the unjust sentence of a lower tribunal.[5]

The complaint of nullity (*querela nullitatis*) is essentially a remedy against a sentence that is invalid though possessed of the appearance of validity. It is a judicial petition asking that the sentence be declared null inasmuch as it labors under substantial defect.[6] The complaint of nullity is always prosecuted before the judge who pronounced the sentence,[7] except under certain circumstances when it may be joined with appeal,[8] and then the complaint will be heard by the judge of the next instance who receives the appeal.[9]

One of the most distinctive phases of the office of the *Defensor Vinculi* is that which embraces his rights and duties in connection with the interposition of the appeal from a sentence declaring a marriage null. The distinctiveness of the duty lies in the fact that he is obliged to appeal from the first sentence for nullity regardless of how evident the case may be.[10] This obligation derives from the principle that requires two conformable sentences before a case involving the validity of marriage attains the status of *quasi-res iudicata.*[11] These cases and others involving the status of persons can never attain the true status of *res iudicata.*[12]

Translated into practical terms this means that although the

[5] Connolly, *Appeals,* pp. 3, 4; Schmalzgrueber, lib. II, Tit. xxvii, n. 1; Wernz-Vidal, *Jus Canonicum,* VI, n. 600, I and II; Roberti, *De Processibus,* II, n. 460.

[6] Wernz-Vidal, *Jus Canonicum,* VI, n. 614; Roberti, *De Processibus,* II, nn. 489 and 490.

[7] Canons 1893, 1895; Roberti, *De Processibus,* II, n. 496.

[8] Canon 1895.

[9] Canon 1895; Roberti, *De Processibus,* II, n. 496.

[10] Canon 1986.

[11] Canon 1987; Benedict XIV, const., *Dei Miseratione,* November 3, 1741, n. 14—*Fontes,* n. 318.

[12] Canon 1903.

persons involved can remarry after the second uncontested sentence confirming the nullity of the previous marriage, nevertheless the case may be later reopened if new evidence or documents have been found.[13]

Article II

The *Defensor Vinculi* and His Obligation to Appeal from a Sentence for Nullity

The *Defensor Vinculi* has both the right and the duty to interpose this appeal. Under certain circumstances he may refrain from the exercise of his right if he believes the sentence to be just. Under other circumstances the duty to interpose the appeal is mandatory.[14]

The *Defensor Vinculi* is always bound to appeal from the first sentence declaring a marriage null and void. If he fails to perform his duty in this regard he may be forced to do so by the judge.[15]

The *Defensor Vinculi* cannot appeal from the first sentence declaring the marriage valid. His right to appeal is based only on his office, and hence his rights cannot extend beyond the scope of his duties as *Defensor Vinculi*. Certainly, it is not his duty as *Defensor Vinculi* to appeal from a sentence declaring the marriage valid, on the contrary he would be acting in absolute contradiction to his official obligations in so doing. Not being a party personally concerned in the action but an official, he may only appeal when commissioned by law to do so. Not being so authorized, he not only should not appeal, but he cannot appeal from the first definitive sentence for validity.[16]

13 Canon 1989.

14 Canons 1879, 1986.

15 Canon 1986; De Becker, *De Matrimonio* (1931 edit.), p. 278; Grandclaude, *Jus Canonicum*, I, p. 162; Laurentius, *Praelectiones I. C.*, n. 696; Mansella, *De Impedimentis*, p. 214; Muñiz, *Procedimientos Ecclesiasticos*, III, p. 466; Sipos, *Enchiridion*, p. 883; Wernz-Vidal, *Jus Canonicum*, V, n. 703.

16 "Itaque si a Iudice pro Matrimonii validitate iudicabitur et nullus sit, qui appellet, ipse (Defensor Matrimonii) etiam ab appellatione se abstineat;

It would not be reasonable for the *Defensor Vinculi* to appeal from the first sentence for validity. He has been successful in the exercise of his duties before the court, the validity of the marriage has been upheld, and therefore can have no just complaint against the sentence. The exercise of the right to appeal implies that the one exercising the right has suffered at least partial setback in the prosecution of his case before the court, for the right is given to the "*Pars quae aliqua sententia se gravatam putat* . . ."[17]

The cause for the validity of the marriage defended by the *Defensor Vinculi* certainly does not suffer defeat by reason of a sentence declaring the marriage valid. Neither do canons 1986 and 1987 which define the duties of the *Defensor Vinculi* in connection with appeals, impose on him the duty or grant him the right to appeal from a sentence for the validity of the marriage.

There is no way in which a sentence for validity can hurt the cause of the *Defensor Vinculi,* no matter how poor the reasoning behind the decision may be.

It is quite possible to imagine a case in which important evidence comes to the notice of the *Defensor Vinculi* after the favorable termination of the trial, evidence that would render the validity of the marriage absolutely certain. Would the *Defensor Vinculi* be empowered or bound to appeal from a sentence for validity under these circumstances?

The arguments given above force the answer to be negative. However, by reason of his office the *Defensor Vinculi* would be bound to some kind of action in the matter, but not by strict letter of the law, for it applies only to the *Defensor* when taking part in judicial proceedings.

The *Defensor Vinculi* has not a strict right to appeal under these circumstances, as an official he does not suffer defeat by reason of the sentence; he cannot employ the complaint of nullity for the sentence is valid.

idque etiam servetur, si a Iudice secundae instantiae pro validitate Matrimonii fuerit iudicatum, postquam Iudex primae instantiae de illius nullitate Sententiam pronunciaverat"; Benedict XIV, const., *Dei Miseratione,* November 3, 1741, n. 8—*Fontes,* n. 318.

[17] Canon 1879.

This case, however, while very alarming considered in the abstract, in actual practice offers no serious difficulty.

In the first place the party seeking the declaration of nullity, having the right to appeal from the sentence for validity in order to discern the truth in the matter, is not impeded from so doing, for the case has not yet been placed in the status of *quasi-res iudicata,* since two conformable sentences have not been pronounced.

The *Defensor Vinculi* of first instance could, if necessary, easily bring the newly acquired evidence to the attention of the *Defensor* of second instance. Indeed, he would be bound by his oath of office to do so, for while the persons of the *Defensors* in question are different, the office is the same.

If the party seeking the declaration of nullity were so remiss in the prosecution of his or her rights, that no appeal was made, then the declaration for validity would stand, and the indissolubility of the marriage would be as secure as if it were never contested. In neither event is it imperilled by the failure of the *Defensor* to interpose an appeal.

The obligation of the *Defensor Vinculi* to appeal from the first sentence for nullity is mandatory, regardless of how evident the nullity of the marriage may be, as long as the case does not fall under the exceptions listed in canon 1990. Whenever the nullity of a marriage is claimed in the solemn process, in the event of a sentence so declaring, the *Defensor Vinculi* must appeal.[18]

The *Defensor* also is obliged to interpose his appeal against the sentence declaring the marriage null regardless of whether one of the parties acting as defendant also interposes an appeal.[19]

Vlaming maintains that the *Defensor Vinculi* is excused from the obligation to interpose an appeal when the defendant in the case does so.[20] However, no support for this view can be found in the Code or in the light of closer examination of the effects of the exercise of the right to appeal by the *Defensor Vinculi* under these circumstances.

[18] Canon 1986, " . . . provocare debet."

[19] Connolly, Appeals, p. 65; *Instructio Austriaca,* nn. 181, 183—*Collectio Lacensis,* V, n. 1302 ff.

[20] *Praelectiones Juris Matrimonii,* II, n. 802.

It might seem at first sight to be a useless duplication of effort for the *Defensor Vinculi* to interpose an appeal from the sentence for nullity simultaneously with one of the parties. A brief consideration of the facts however, will easily serve to discover reasons to overthrow this first impression.

If one of the parties in the case were to interpose an appeal, he or she may easily desert the appeal. This would not be known until the month's period of grace for the prosecution of the appeal had expired, and hence the trial would be subjected to unwarranted delay.

The appeal of the *Defensor Vinculi* on the other hand can never be deserted, except in the event of the dissolution of the marriage in question by death, in which event the *Defensor Vinculi* is neither empowered nor obliged to continue the prosecution of the appeal.[21]

The *Defensor Vinculi* is not only obliged to interpose an appeal from the first sentence for nullity, but he is also obliged to do so within the period fixed by law.[22]

This period of time for the interposition of the appeal is fixed by law as ten days.[23] The ten-day period may not be shortened or
prolata est intra decem dies a notitia publicationis sententiae."
lengthened by the judge,[24] nor may he accept an appeal after the ten days have legally elapsed.[25]

The ten days must also be ten days of useful time (*tempus utile*), time during which the right to appeal has not been impeded. The ten days, therefore, do not begin to run until the first day after the notification of the publication of the sentence, and do not cease until the end of the last day.[26]

This period is absolutely peremptory in the ordinary trial, that is, at the termination of the period the right to appeal can no longer be deemed to exist.[27]

[21] *Cf. Decisiones, S. R. Rotae,* XIV (1922), *Decisio,* xix.

[22] " . . . intra legitimum tempus, ad superius tribunal provocare debet"—Canon 1986.

[23] Canon 1881—"Appellatio interponi debet coram iudice a quo sententia

[24] Canon 1634, § 1; Wernz-Vidal, *Jus Canonicum,* nn. 85, 610; Roberti, *De Processibus,* I, n. 185.

[25] Noval, *De Processibus,* n. 229; Wernz-Vidal, *Jus Canonicum,* VI, 185.

[26] Connolly, *Appeals,* p. 103 ff.

[27] Wernz-Vidal, *Jus Canonicum,* VI, nn. 185, 610; Roberti, *De Processibus,* II, n. 478, p. 212; Connolly, *Appeals,* p. 103.

In those cases in which the *Defensor Vinculi* is bound by the mandatory duty to appeal, failure to interpose the appeal within the stated time, terminates neither the duty nor the right of the *Defensor Vinculi* to appeal.[28]

This is indicated by the very language of canon 1986, which declares that if the *Defensor Vinculi* fails to appeal within the time fixed by law,[29] he is to be compelled to do so by the judge.[30] The wording of the canon clearly states that when the *Defensor* has not interposed his appeal within the ten-day period fixed by the law, the judge then is to force him to do so, a clear admission that such action is possible.

The argument derived from this canon regards only the mandatory appeal of the *Defensor Vinculi* from the first sentence for nullity, a duty which the *Defensor* cannot yield or renounce.[31]

The nature of the *fatalia legis* in connection with the appeal of the *Defensor* from a second sentence for nullity presents another problem, since the *Defensor* is free to refrain from interposing this appeal according to the dictates of his conscience.

It is quite evident that the time fixed by canon 1886 for the interposition of the appeal, is fixed to terminate the right, and not merely to expedite its use. The *fatalia legis,* as these peremptory periods are termed, are not generally applied to the exercise of duties, and hence it would seem that the *Defensor* is excused from the peremptory effect of this period even when interposing the optional appeal from the second sentence for nullity.

It is quite evident that any attempt to allow the peremptory effect of this term on the appeal of the *Defensor Vinculi* from the second sentence for nullity, is tantamount to a claim that while the mandatory appeal from the first sentence for nullity is a duty, the optional appeal from a second sentence for nullity is only a right.

This is manifestly incorrect. The *Defensor Vinculi* certainly has a duty to appeal from the first sentence for nullity, but he is equally bound in duty to appeal from the second sentence for nullity if he

28 Canon 1986, 1; *Instructio Austriaca,* n. 184.

29 Canon 1881.

30 " . . . et si negligat officium suum implere, compellatur auctoritate iudicis."

31 A Coronata, *De Processibus,* p. 324, n. 1409, 1.

believes that the grounds for the sentence were insufficient or doubtful. He is then bound in conscience to interpose the appeal by virtue of his office, and his oath. Such an obligation can hardly be regarded simply as a duty. Hence if the *Defensor Vinculi* is exempted from the peremptory effects of the *fatalia legis* in the interposition of the appeal from the first sentence for nullity, because the *fatalia legis* terminate only the exercise of rights, and do not apply to the fulfillment of duties, the same reasoning should also exempt him from their peremptory effect in the interposition of his appeal from the second sentence for nullity. If the *Defensor* believes that the appeal is warranted, he has no mere right to appeal, he has a solemn duty to appeal.[82]

The instruction of the Sacred Congregation of the Holy Office sent to the Oriental Bishops in the year 1883, seems to give support to this view. It states that although the *Defensor Vinculi* is not bound by the *fatalia legis* fixed for the interposition of appeals, he should none the less ordinarily observe them.[83]

The mere fact that the immediately following phrase states that the judge may force the *Defensor Vinculi* to interpose his appeal within the time fixed by law, does not of necessity imply that the appeal concerned is the obligatory appeal from the first sentence for nullity. The judge may know from past experience that this particular *Defensor Vinculi* habitually fails to interpose his appeals on time.

The *Instructio Austriaca* a semi-official commentary on the law, and of great authority states:

> Relate ad appellationes, quas interponere Defensor Matrimonii muneris sui ratione obligatur, nulli habentur dies fatales.[84]

It is patently in full agreement with the arguments stated above, since the *Defensor* is as equally bound by reason of his office when he appeals from the first sentence for nullity as he is when he feels that he should appeal from the second sentence for nullity. In both

[82] *Th. pr. QS.*, LXXXIII (1930), 597, 598.

[83] S. C. S. Off., Instr. (*ad Ep. Rituum Orient.*), a 1883, Tit. iv, n. 25—*Fontes*, n. 1076.

[84] N. 184; *Collectio Lacensis*, V, n. 1302 ff.

cases he acts by reason of his office and the reasons that excuse him in the one should also excuse him in the other case.

It is well to note that the claim cannot be made that the Holy See has repudiated or corrected the law as stated in those instructions which belong to the same family as that sent to the Orientals in the year 1883. An instruction was sent to the Bishops of the United States in the same year, 1883 through the Sacred Congregation of the Propagation of the Faith, that was identical in essentials with the one sent to the Orientals.[35]

An instruction was sent to China in the year 1929 for the regulation of matrimonial trials. It is interesting to note that paragraph 25 of this instruction is in verbal agreement with that of the year 1883.[36]

While it is true that these instructions grant exceptions from the common law of the Church, yet when these exceptions do occur, they are quite evident, being called for by reasons of time, place or condition of the people for whom they are intended. While granting important concessions, these instructions for the most part are made up of detailed explanations of the common law of the Church. The section under discussion is an instance of this practice. These instructions for the most part are meant for those who fight in the First Line of Christ's Army, and consequently have neither sufficient time nor sufficient books at their disposal to study the law of the Church fully. In view of their position the Church from time to time sends them official commentaries on the law, as well as exemptions from its full rigor.

It is for this reason that the greatest confidence can be placed in an interpretation of the law based on these instructions.

The *Instructio Austriaca* is also well worthy of confidence, for although a private document, it was drawn up at the recommendation of the Holy See for the use of the Church in Austria.

It would seem therefore that the opinion giving to the *Defensor Vinculi* complete exemption from the peremptory effect of the *fatalia*

[35] Gasparri, *De Matrimonio*, II, p. 276.

[36] S. C. de Prop. Fid., Instr., *Pro Causis Matrimonialibus in Sinis,* February 18, 1929, n. 25—Payen, *De Matrimonio,* II, in appendix; and S. C. S. Off., Instr. (*ad Ep. Rituum Orient.*), a. 1883—*Fontes,* n. 1076.

legis enjoys sufficient intrinsic and extrinsic credibility to render it truly probable. Yet most authors while willing to grant this exemption to the *Defensor* in connection with the mandatory appeal from the first sentence for validity, are unwilling to go so far as to extend the exemption to the *Defensor Vinculi* in the interposition of his appeal from a second sentence for nullity.[87]

Perhaps they are influenced in this connection by the clause of canon 1987, which permits the parties to contract new marriages, if an appeal has not been interposed within the ten-day period following the declaration of the sentence. Yet a marriage case never becomes *res iudicata* when the bond of marriage itself is involved, and the mere fact that the parties are free to remarry does not touch the merits of the question in any way. This may be considered to be a purely practical regulation.

A Coronata states that even after the lapse of the time of the *fatalia legis,* the *Defensor* or one of the parties may interpose an appeal if they have discovered new evidence or new documents. This statement is not strictly concerned with the question under discussion, which is, does the appeal of the *Defensor* fail, if not interposed within the ten-day period? Any case involving personal status may be reopened at any time if new evidence or new arguments are discovered. The case implied by A Coronata is ruled by canons 1989 and 1903 which lift from all personal status cases the effects of *res iudicata.* The case under discussion is ruled only by the law of appeals. The finding of new evidence after a second sentence in matrimonial cases would entitle the case to be tried again in first instance, or before the Rota sitting as a court of first instance.[88]

Therefore the remarks of this author are not pertinent to this question, they concern the request for the reexamination of a case, rather than the interposition of an appeal.

The conclusion to the discussion seems to be quite clear. The *Defensor* is exempted from the peremptory effect of the *fatalia legis* in the interposition of his appeal from the first sentence for nullity.

[87] Haring, in *Th. pr. QS.*, LXXXIII (1930), 597, 598; Roberti, in *Apollinaris,* II (1929), 516, 517; A Coronata, *De Processibus,* p. 324, n .1410, 2°, a., and p. 434, n. 1498; Wernz-Vidal, *Jus Canonicum,* VI, n. 610.

[88] Canons 1989, 1903.

He is likewise exempted when he makes the optional appeal from the second sentence for nullity. In other words his action would be valid after the lapse of the time fixed by law for the placing of the act. In both appeals, the mandatory and the optional, he is bound to observe the *fatalia legis* to the extent, that to ignore them without reason would render his actions illicit.

It is well to bear in mind that the *Defensor Vinculi* is essentially a sort of Commonwealth Attorney and in court he defends not any private interest, but the law whenever the bond of marriage is involved. Is it likely that the law wishes to limit the rights of its own vindicator in any way? It might be claimed that there is danger of the *Defensor Vinculi* abusing these rights. This criticism disappears when it is considered that the legal qualifications demanded in the holder of this office, require as *Defensor Vinculi* a man no more likely to abuse his rights than the judge himself.

In view of the fact of the acceptance of the view that the *Defensor Vinculi* is bound by the ten fatal days in interposing his appeal from the second conformable sentence for nullity by many authors, it will be useful to summarize briefly the legal interruptions that will estop the running of the ten days.

This period of ten days is a period of useful time (*tempus utile*) that is time during which there is no legal impediment to the exercise of the right.[39]

Canons 1773 and 1885 state the reasons capable of interrupting and abating this period. It is quite possible for the office of the *Defensor Vinculi* to become vacant during this period either by death, resignation, dismissal or renunciation. In this event the *tempus utile* would be interrupted and would not begin to run again until the office had been filled.[40]

[39] Canon 35; *cf.* Connolly, *Appeals,* p. 104.

[40] Roberti, *De Processibus,* II, 310; Connolly, *Appeals,* p. 109; Wernz-Vidal, *Ius Canonicum,* VI, n. 411.

Article III

Some Special Applications of the Duty of the *Defensor Vinculi* in Connection with Appeals

The best summary of the duty of the *Defensor Vinculi* in connection with the interposing of appeals is to be found in the Code of Canon Law itself.

First Principle

The *Defensor Vinculi* in the solemn matrimonial process is always bound to appeal from the first sentence for nullity regardless of the instance in which it has been received.[41]

Second Principle

After a second sentence for nullity the *Defensor Vinculi* is free to appeal or not, entirely depending on whether he believes the sentence to be in accord with truth or at variance with it.[42]

It has been previously pointed out that the *Defensor Vinculi* cannot appeal from a sentence for validity, and this is equally true if two sentences for validity have been returned, nor would the *Defensor Vinculi* have any real reason for doing so.

In the event that a sentence for validity is received in second instance after one in first instance for nullity, the *Defensor* is likewise unable to appeal.[43]

The *Defensor* in first instance obeyed the law of canon 1986 when he appealed from the sentence for nullity. The *Defensor* in second instance brought the case to a successful termination, and he has no need to have recourse to a remedy against the sentence, since the cause for validity has been sustained, and has not been prejudiced

[41] Canon 1986—"A prima sententia quae matrimonii nullitatem declaraverit, vinculi defensor, . . . ad superius tribunal provocare debet; . . . "

[42] Canon 1987—"Post secundam sententiam, quae matrimonii nullitatem confirmaverit, si defensor vinculi in gradu appellationis pro sua conscientia non crediderit esse appellandum, . . ."

[43] *Cf.* Lanier, *Guide Pratique de la Procedure Matrimoniale,* p. 31.

in any way.[44] Nor can any harm come to the status of the marriage through the abstinence of the *Defensor Vinculi* from appealing. The parties cannot remarry, though it is indeed true they may appeal, but in this event the *Defensor Vinculi* of the next instance would take up the defense of the marriage, and this is exactly what would have happened if the *Defensor Vinculi* himself had interposed the appeal.

In view of the fact that the law of the Code gives no certain indication that it intends to change the former law, only one conclusion is possible, namely that the *Defensor* may never appeal from a sentence declaring a marriage valid.[45]

The reason for the above conclusion is to be found in the following statement in the constitution *"Dei Miseratione"* of Benedict XIV:

> Itaque si a Iudice pro Matrimonii validitate iudicabitur, et nullis sit, qui appellet, ipse [the defensor] etiam ab appellatione se abstineat; idque etiam servetur, si a Iudice secundae instantiae pro validitate Matrimonii fuerit iudicatum, postquam Iudex primae instantiae de illius nullitate Sententiam pronunciaverat; . . . [46]

The doctrine of the Benedictine Constitution was later reiterated by the instruction of the Sacred Congregation of the Council of August 22, 1840, and confirmed again in the instruction sent to the Oriental Bishops and the United States in the year 1883.[47] Evidence of the fact that the Code has effected no change in this legislation is shown by the fact that the recent instruction sent to China for the regulation of marriage trials is in literal agreement with the previous instruction of the Holy Office covering the same matter sent to the Orientals on this point.[48]

In evaluating the force of these pronouncements it must be kept in mind that in commenting on these points these instructions are

[44] Canon 1879—"Pars quae aliqua sententia se gravatam putat, . . . et defensor vinculi . . . , ius habet a sententia appellandi . . "

[45] Canon 6, 2° and 4°.

[46] N. 8—*Fontes,* n. 318.

[47] S. C. S. Off., Instr. (*ad Ep. Rituum Orient.*), a 1883, nn. 25 and 30—*Fontes,* n. 1076.

[48] S. C. de Prop. Fid., Instr., *Pro Causis Matrimonialibus in Sinis,* February 18, 1929, nn. 25 and 30—Payen, *De Matrimonio,* in appendix.

not explaining idults, but the common law of the Church. The Church cannot be considered as departing completely from the ordinary law of the trial in these instructions, as is evident from even a casual reading.

The opinion above stated that the *Defensor Vinculi* should never appeal from a sentence of validity is not shared by all authors.[49]

The commentary of Wernz-Vidal concedes to both the parties and the *Defensor Vinculi* the right to appeal when the first sentence was for nullity and the second for validity.[50]

This opinion does not seem to be logical. In the first place such action on the part of the *Defensor Vinculi* is prohibited by the constitution "*Dei Miseratione*" of Benedict XIV.[51] In the second place such appeal on the part of the *Defensor Vinculi* has no practical effect on the progress of the case for validity. If the *Defensor Vinculi* interposes this appeal, the case goes to the next instance, and the *Defensor* of that Curia is called in to defend the cause for validity. If the plaintiff appeals, the case goes to the next instance, and the *Defensor* is likewise called in. If the plaintiff fails to exercise the right to appeal, the case is terminated successfully as far as the *Defensor Vinculi* is concerned with the validity of the marriage unimpaired. Appeal on the part of the *Defensor Vinculi* under these circumstances is clearly a useless proceeding, and the law does not regard useless actions with a friendly eye.

As has been pointed out in a prior part of this discussion the right of the *Defensor Vinculi* to appeal derives from the mandate of his office. His office can hardly be regarded as obliging him to place a useless action, or to authorize him to execute such an act. Furthermore he is not the *pars gravata* and therefore not entitled to appeal by the basic law as stated in canon 1879.

Cappello states that if the two sentences disagree, both the parties and the *Defensor* may appeal, and that in the event that the last sentence was for nullity the *Defensor* must appeal.[52]

[49] Wernz-Vidal, *Jus Canonicum,* V, n. 703; Cappello, *De Sacramentis,* III, p. 940, n. 887; Payen, *De Matrimonio,* III, n. 2715, 3.

[50] Wernz-Vidal, *loc. cit.*

[51] N. 8—*Fontes,* n. 318.

[52] Cappello, *De Sacramentis,* III, p. 940, n. 887.

This opinion is only partially true in the light of the above stated opinion. It is indeed true that if the last of two discordant sentences pronounces for nullity, the *Defensor Vinculi* is obliged to appeal. In this case he is appealing from the first sentence for nullity, and this is the mandatory duty of the *Defensor Vinculi.*[53] But it will be equally evident in the light of the previously stated opinion, that where the last of these discordant sentences finds for validity, then the *Defensor* is neither obliged nor authorized to appeal.

Cappello proceeds to present another slightly different case, in which a sentence for validity is received after the pronouncement of two sentences for nullity. This case does not fall within the scope of this dissertation, inasmuch as it concerns an appeal from third to fourth instance, which would bring the case before the *Rota* according to the common law of the Church, but even before the *Rota* the *Defensor Vinculi* would not be empowered to appeal from a sentence for validity.[54]

Cappello however, is by no means alone in this opinion, for most of the authors who treat the matter with any degree of thoroughness agree with him.[55]

Nevertheless the only conclusion possible after close investigation of this question is that the appeal of the *Defensor Vinculi* from a sentence of validity following a sentence for nullity, is not only forbidden by the former law, but also useless since it adds nothing to the security of the validity of the sacrament of Marriage.

According to the second principle governing the exercise of the right of appeal by the *Defensor Vinculi* as found in the Code,[56] the *Defensor Vinculi* is bound to appeal from a second sentence confirming the nullity of the marriage only when he believes that there is a

[53] Canon 1986; Benedict XIV, const., *Dei Miseratione,* nn. 8, 14—*Fontes,* n. 318.

[54] It is the opinion of the writer that the opinion above stated is just as valid before the *Rota* as it is under the common law by reason of the content of *Regula* 108, n. 4, of the *Regulae Servandae in Iudiciis apud S. R. Rotae Tribunal.*

[55] A Coronata, *De Processibus,* p. 434, n. 1498, footnote 4; Chelodi, *Jus Matrimoniale,* p. 179; Wernz-Vidal, *Jus Canonicum,* V, n. 703; Payen, *De Matrimonio,* III, p. 526, n. 2715, 3.

[56] Canon 1987.

reasonable probability that the marriage is actually valid. This is self-evident and is not controverted.[57]

Under these circumstances the *Defensor Vinculi* should not appeal merely as a matter of course. It would be unjust for him to act in this fashion, for then his intention would be simply to prevent the parties from receiving something that they have a right in justice to receive—the sentence of the court.

Because of the presumption of validity that an apparently valid marriage enjoys, it would be difficult to demand grave reason for the justification of the appeal of the *Defensor Vinculi*. He would be sufficiently justified in appealing if he had a reasonable doubt as to the verity of the sentence for nullity.

In another sense any conviction on the part of the *Defensor Vinculi* that the marriage is in truth valid, would always constitute grave reason, for to allow the sentence to stand would expose the parties to serious sin, and expose the sacrament of Marriage to abuse.

Article IV

The Prosecution of the Appeal of the *Defensor Vinculi*

The act of appeal is touched by two peremptory periods of time within which the right is to be exercised. The one is the ten-day period during which the appeal is to be interposed before the judge who pronounced the sentence, the other a period of one month during which the appeal must be prosecuted before the judge to whom the appeal is directed. The ten-day period during which the appeal must be interposed has already been fully treated in this discussion.

The statement of the law that rules the one month period within which the appeal is to be prosecuted is found in canon 1883.

This period is also one of the *fatalia legis,* and is, therefore, a period of time set up by law, for the exercise of a right and after

[57] Wernz-Vidal, *Jus Canonicum,* V, n. 703; De Becker, *De Matrimonio* (1931 edit.), p. 277; Cappello, *De Sacramentis,* III, p. 940, n. 887; Vermeersch-Creusen, *Epitome,* III, n. 295; Payen, *De Matrimonio,* III, p. 526, n. 2715, 3, 2°; Lanier, *Guide Pratique de la Procedure Matrimoniale,* p. 30; Benedict XIV, const., *Dei Miseratione,* November 3, 1741, 11—*Fontes,* n. 318.

the expiration of which the right is lost. In other words if a month passes without the prosecution of the appeal before the court of appeal, the appeal is considered to be deserted.[58]

In what then does prosecution of the appeal consist? Prosecution of an appeal consists in the invocation of the help of the appellate tribunal in the form of a petition which is accompanied with an authentic exemplar of the sentence pronounced in the lower court.[59] The petition here mentioned is the petition of appeal that was exhibited to the lower court for the interposition of the appeal, or an authentic copy of the *acta* describing the interposition of the oral appeal.

The question that immediately arises is the one that is intimately bound up with the ten-day period for the interposing of the appeal.

Does the *Defensor Vinculi* lose his right to urge his appeal if he fails to prosecute it within a month before the court of the next instance?

When the *Defensor* appeals from the first sentence for nullity he certainly cannot lose his right to urge the appeal even if he fails to prosecute within the month fixed by the law. This is quite evident from the tenor of the Pre-Code legislation concerned with the time fixed by law for appeal. Certainly too, if he can interpose the appeal after the period of time fixed by law has elapsed he may also urge the appeal after the lapse of the time fixed for the prosecution of the appeal, for both apply to different aspects of the same act—that of appeal.

The opinion adopted in connection with the thirty-day period for the prosecution of the appeal will be in agreement with the stand taken concerning the ten-day period for the interposition of the appeal.

Therefore this period of a month is certainly lacking in peremptory effect when it concerns the mandatory appeal of the *Defensor Vinculi* from the first sentence for nullity. It is also probably lacking in peremptory effect when it touches the appeal of the *Defensor* from a second sentence for nullity.

[58] Canon 1886.

[59] Canon 1884, § 1; Roberti, *De Processibus,* II, n. 479.

Since the *Defensor Vinculi* is strictly bound to interpose an appeal from the first sentence declaring a marriage null, it necessarily follows that the *Defensor* of the higher instance is likewise strictly bound to prosecute such an appeal.

It also follows from this conclusion that the *Defensor* of third instance is free to abandon an appeal interposed against a second sentence declaring a marriage null, whenever he is of the opinion that the prosecution of the appeal would be useless, since his obligation is similar to that of the *Defensor* of the lower instance. This conclusion is confirmed by the action of the *Defensor* before the *Rota* in abandoning two cases during the year 1933.[60] In both cases the Rota declared the appeals to be deserted, in view of abandonment by the *Defensor Vinculi* of the *Rota*. It is also interesting to note that the *Defensor Vinculi* of the *Rota* is bound by the common law of the Church, the Code.[61]

Article V

The Meaning of the Phrase "Two Conformable Sentences" in the Legislation Dealing with the *Defensor Vinculi*

Cases that involve the personal status of individuals never become *res iudicata* in the strict sense,[62] and marriage cases are among those included in this category.[63] These cases do, however, attain a status of *quasi-res iudicata* after the declaration of two conformable sentences.[64] This principle is of the greatest importance to the *Defensor Vinculi* because he is freed of the obligation to interpose an appeal against a sentence for nullity, only after the pronouncement of two conformable sentences.[65] It is therefore of the utmost importance to determine just what is meant

[60] *AAS,* XXVI (1934), Causa VI, p. 126; Causa XVI, p. 127.

[61] *Reg. Serv. S. R. Rotae,* n. 108, 4°; Canon 1555, §§ 1, 2.

[62] Canon 1903.

[63] Canon 1989.

[64] Canon 1903; Benedict XIV, const., *Dei Miseratione,* November 3, 1741, n. 11—*Fontes,* n. 318.

[65] Canon 1987; Benedict XIV, const., *Dei Miseratione,* November 3, 1741, nn. 11, 14—*Fontes,* n. 318.

by two conformable sentences. Suppose the two sentences declared the marriage to be invalid, but on different grounds. Would these sentences be conformable? The answer must of necessity be a negative one. The legislation involved in this question is clearly the same as that set forth in the constitution *"Dei Miseratione"* of Benedict XIV.[66] This is the most evident source of the law under discussion. True, the regulation that marriage cases never become *res iudicata* is traceable to a much earlier law,[67] but the Benedictine Constitution certainly and authentically states the law in unmistakable terms.

Before going further into the discussion it must be admitted that this question could arise only under one set of circumstances. The case of necessity pictures a court of first instance granting a sentence of nullity, but only on one of the two grounds alleged. The case is then appealed by the *Defensor* to second instance, where the court finds the marriage invalid, but also on only one of the two grounds alleged, the one which the court of first instance would not admit to be cause of the nullity of the marriage. Thus two sentences have validly been handed down declaring the marriage null, but on different grounds.[68]

The general rule governing the acquisition of the status of *quasi-res iudicata* by matrimonial cases is to be found in section 11 of the *"Dei Miseratione"* of Benedict XIV, in the following words:

> . . . si secunda sententia alteri conformis fuerit, hoc est, si in secunda, aeque ac in prima, nullum ac irritum matrimonium iudicatum fuerit, et ab ea Pars, vel Defensor pro sua conscientia non crediderit appellandum, vel appellationem interpositam prosequendam minime censuerit: in potestate, et arbitrio Coniugum sit novas nuptias contrahere;

It is evident that this statement of the law does not sufficiently explain itself to solve the difficulty under discussion. The Pope, however, explains his meaning more fully in n. 14 of the same constitution when he says:

66 *Fontes,* n. 318.

67 C. 7, X, *de sententia et re iudicata,* II, 27.

68 *Cf. Periodica,* XX (1931), 20 ff.

> . . . nolentes omnino, ut ullo in casu matrimonii vinculum dissolutum censeatur, nisi duo iudicata vel resolutiones, aut sententiae penitus similes, et conformes, . . .

It is clear from this quotation that Pope Benedict demanded that the two sentences be identical, fully conformable. In other words the sentences must be in agreement at least on all essential points.

In connection with this discussion it must be kept in mind that a sentence does not simply state that the marriage was found to be null, it must also give with the decision the reasons both in fact and law upon which the sentence was based, and this under pain of nullity.[69]

In short the sentence must be in agreement with the *libellus* or petition with which the trial was opened.[70]

That the reasons both in fact and in law are an essential part of the sentence is indicated by the fact that they must be included under pain of nullity.[71]

If two sentences differ in essential features they can hardly be regarded as "*conformes.*" By no means are they "*penitus similes.*"

Nor can it be claimed that the Code changed the former law with regard to this question.[72]

True, the Code has recognized exceptions from the Benedictine regulations, but these exceptions were substantially the same before the Code,[73] but nevertheless these exceptions have not destroyed the force of the general rules derived from the Benedictine Laws. These were exceptions from the law granted by the law itself and confirmed by the Code. They no more destroy the

[69] Canons 1873, § 1, 3°; 1874, § 4; Roberti, *De Processibus,* II, n. 456; Wernz-Vidal, *Jus Canonicum,* VI, p. 540, II.

[70] C. 6, X, *de arb.,* I, 43; C. 6, X, *de iudiciis,* II, 1; C. 11, X, *de trans.,* I, 36; C. 1, X, *de dolo et contumac.,* II, 14; Wernz-Vidal, *Jus Canonicum,* p. 540, n. 592, II.

[71] Canon 1894, 2°.

[72] Canons 1903, 1986, 1987, 1989; Benedict XIV, const., *Dei Miseratione,* November 2, 1741, nn. 11, 14—*Fontes,* n. 318.

[73] S. C. S. Off., decr., June 5, 1889—*Fontes,* n. 1118; *cf.* canons 1990, 1991, 1992.

general law, than does a matrimonial dispensation destroy the law of the impediment from which it dispenses.

There has been no real change in the law after the Code, hence canons 1903, 1987, and 1989 must be understood in the light of the Pre-Code law.[74]

Therefore in order that two sentences for nullity be conformable, it is necessary that at least they agree in the causes upon which the nullity was based. The meaning of the constitution *"Dei Miseratione,"* is very clear, and therefore the two sentences now, as well as then must be fully conformable in order for the case to attain to the status of *quasi-res iudicata.*

In other words the *Defensor Vinculi* would be bound to appeal even if two sentences were handed down declaring the marriage null but on different grounds, even in a case where the *Defensor* was convinced that the marriage was in reality null. He has no other alternative but to regard the last of two such sentences as a first sentence for nullity, since it does not confirm the prior sentence,[75] and therefore the appeal of the *Defensor Vinculi* is obligatory.[76]

Article VI

The *Defensor Vinculi* and the Complaint of Nullity (*Querela Nullitatis*)

The *Defensor Vinculi* may also have recourse to the use of the Complaint of Nullity, one of the two ordinary remedies against an unfavorable and invalid sentence.

This is an action by which one of the parties to the trial contends that the promulgated sentence is null in as much as it suffers from substantial defect.[77]

A sentence may become null in two ways. If the sentence has been promulgated by a judge absolutely incompetent, or in a case in which one of the parties does not enjoy the right to stand in

[74] Canon 6, 2°.
[75] Canon 1987.
[76] Canon 1986.
[77] Reiffenstuel, II, 28, 23; A Coronata, *De Processibus,* p. 334, n. 1417.

court, or in which someone has acted in the name of another without the necessary mandate; in all these cases the sentence is irrevocably null and void.[78] The sentence null because of these reasons can never be rendered valid by any subsequent act. Against it there may be obtained a perpetual exception, which exception is an action that may be exercised before the court which gave the sentence even in nonpersonal status cases, for a period of thirty years. Of course the limitation of the exercise of this type of complaint of nullity to thirty years will not concern the *Defensor Vinculi* for marriage cases in which validity is concerned are bound by no such limits as these, since they never become *res iudicata*.[79]

The *Defensor Vinculi* may institute this action whenever he discovers the sentence labors under any of the aforementioned defects.[80] If successful there will be no necessity of further action on his part.

The second type of sentence against which a complaint of nullity may be entered is a sentence that is null, but which may be corrected and thus rendered valid. This type of nullity may derive from several factors, among them, lack of citation, absence of the motives in law and in fact from the sentence itself, defect in signature or date of the sentence itself.[81]

The *Defensor Vinculi* is also empowered to enter the complaint of nullity against a sentence suffering from this type of defect.[82]

Ordinarily it will be the usual practice for the *Defensor Vinculi* to join this action with his appeal, and interpose both within the ten-day period.[83] The complaint of nullity, when exercised against a sentence that is not incurably null, may be prosecuted before the court which gave the sentence any time during a period of three months from the date of publication of the sentence.[84]

[78] Canon 1892, 1°, 2°, 3°.

[79] Canons 1903, 1989.

[80] Canon 1897, § 1; A Coronata, *De Processibus*, p. 338, n. 420, IV; Sipos, *Enchiridion*, p. 883; Wernz-Vidal, *Jus Canonicum*, VI, n. 617.

[81] Canon 1894, 1°, 2°, 3°, 4°.

[82] Canon 1897, § 1; Wernz-Vidal, *Jus Canonicum*, VI, n. 617; A Coronata, *De Processibus*, p. 338, n. 1420, iv.; Sipos, *Enchiridion*, p. 883.

[83] Canon 1895; A Coronata, *De Processibus*, p. 322, n. 1409, 2°.

[84] Canon 1895.

If the complaint of nullity has to be made against a first sentence for nullity, what excuse could the *Defensor* offer for not joining it with his appeal? No judge should permit such a condition to arise. He has a duty to compel the *Defensor* to make the appeal within ten days.[85] What excuse would the judge have to offer for such inaction in the face of certain duty?

It is clear that the *Defensor Vinculi* is not practically concerned with this period of three months, fixed for the making of the *querela nullitatis,* when he is acting against a first sentence for nullity. In addition if he were successful in avoiding the compulsion of the court, he would certainly be acting in an unlawful and unjust manner if he used this action as a means to delay the progress of the case.

Article VII

Some Remarks on the Procedure of Appeal with Reference to the *Defensor Vinculi*

It will be of interest to consider some of the mechanics of the law of interposing an appeal in the light of the rights and duties of the *Defensor Vinculi* in this, the last article of this chapter which was for the most part taken up with the remedies against an unjust or invalid sentence.

There are two distinct acts concerned with the placing of an appeal; the one—interposition of the appeal, the other—prosecution.

It is the *Defensor Vinculi* of the Curia issuing the sentence who interposes the appeal, which he does before the same Curia. By this it is meant that he either declares his appeal before the judge of the court,[86] or presents to the judge a written petition to the same effect. According to the Code this oral declaration of appeal may be used only when the sentence is solemnly pronounced by the judge presiding in court,[87] a procedure that is seldom resorted to

85 Canon 1986.

86 Canon 1882, § 1.

87 Canons 1882, §§ 1, 2; 1877.

in marriage cases. The *Defensor Vinculi,* therefore, will generally be obliged to submit a written petition of appeal.

This judicial petition is directed to the judge who gave the sentence. In the event that the appeal was made orally, it is immediately put in writing by the notary of the court.[88] There is no exact form for the petition of appeal, whether it be oral or written.[89]

The petition of appeal, however, must state certain facts that will at least positively identify the case and the sentence to which it appertains. The petition should therefore at least indicate the judge *a quo* and the judge *ad quem,* explicitly ask the reformation of the sentence, and at least suggest the motive on which the appeal is based. The petition must also be signed by the appellant, for an unsigned document is of no value whatever. The lack of any of these indications with the exception of the signature of the appellant, will not render the petition valueless, as long as no ambiguity exists as to the sentence appealed from, and the court to which it is directed.

The *Defensor Vinculi* certainly does not need to state the motives for his appeal, when he is making the mandatory appeal from the first sentence for nullity. All that is necessary is that he signify his intention to appeal, and give as his motive canon 1986, and clearly identify the sentences he wishes to be corrected and the tribunal to which he directs his appeal.

It may, however, be useful for the *Defensor Vinculi* of the lower court to state clearly the reasons for appealing, when such exist, because in this way he may suggest arguments to the *Defensor Vinculi* of the next instance who will have to prosecute the appeal.

Canon 1884 informs us that for the prosecution of an appeal it suffices that the help of the higher court be invoked, presenting at the same time an authentic exemplar of the impugned sentence. The help of the tribunal may be invoked in the petition of appeal that was presented to the lower court.[90]

The court of the next instance may therefore procede to hear

[88] " . . . statimque ab actuario scriptis redigenda est"—Canon 1882, § 1.

[89] Reiffenstuel, II, 28, 114-123; A Coronata, *De Processibus,* p. 326, n. 1411, iv, a.; Wernz-Vidal, *Jus Canonicum,* VI, n. 611.

[90] *Cf.* Mocnik in *Th. pr. QS,* LXXXV (1932), 142.

a case when the *acta* have been presented to it, without awaiting the formality of the placing of this act.

This matter happens to be of little practical import to the *Defensor Vinculi.* He will ordinarily submit his petition of appeal to the court, and will have little or nothing to do with the transmission of his petition and the *acta* to the superior court. These details are usually handled by the court itself.

However, in view of the content of canon 1884, § 1, the mere transmission of the *acta* does not seem to constitute prosecution of the appeal. The services of the tribunal receiving the appeal should be invoked in order to insure the integrity of the action.[91]

It will be evident, therefore, that the formal prosecution of an appeal by the *Defensor* will seldom be of much importance. The *Defensor Vinculi* of the higher court whose duty it is to urge the appeal interposed by the *Defensor* of the lower court, does not enter the case until the judge has received the *acta* from the lower court. The *Defensor* of the lower court never appears before the higher court, hence the only practical solution will be to transmit to the higher court not only the *acta* but also the appeal of the *Defensor.* Prosecution of the appeal, therefore, will be practically automatic in nearly every instance.

It is the joint duty of both the *Defensor Vinculi* and the presiding judge to see that all these arrangements are properly carried out as is implied by canons 1986, 1890 and 1644.

Strictly speaking the *Defensor Vinculi* himself should see to it that his appeal is presented to the higher court, even though these matters will be taken care of by the Curia itself.

[91] *Jus Pontificium,* IX (1929), 329.

FINAL CONCLUSIONS

THE general purpose of the office of *Defensor Vinculi* is almost self-evident, yet it is one that may be misunderstood very easily.

It is not the duty of the *Defensor Vinculi* simply to strive to thwart the efforts of the party or parties seeking to have a marriage declared null. His function is rather to insure the proper defense of every contested marriage. If he finds that a marriage is certainly invalid, he has no obligation to raise a series of futile and useless objections. He is obliged, however, to cause the marriage to be subjected to the full test of the law, by attacking every defect in the proofs offered for invalidity. He should not make a single motion without a reason. On only one occasion is the *Defensor* obliged to place an act without regard for the merits of the case, and that is when he interposes his mandatory appeal from the first sentence for nullity.

It is especially important for the *Defensor* of second instance to keep in mind the true purpose of his office. He will frequently be active in cases in which a second sentence confirming nullity will be handed down by the court. He should not appeal these cases to Rome, thus subjecting the parties to added delay, unless he has some solid reason for believing the marriage to be in reality valid, or the proof of invalidity defective. In other words he should have reasonable grounds for making this appeal.

A word might also be said about the questions which the *Defensor* is obliged to submit for the use of the court in the examination. Bearing the brunt of the work, he will frequently be obliged to supply the general questions, which serve to identify the witness, but these questions offer no special difficulty.

The particular questions on the other hand are of the greatest importance, since they serve to disclose the evidence to be produced by the witness. These questions should be brief and simple, otherwise the person being examined will either be unable to understand them, or unable to answer them simply.

These questions should not be of the type known as leading questions. Questions of this type are both illicit and useless in canonical procedure. Illicit, because forbidden by the Code; useless, because the person under examination has the right to change the record before signing the testimony.

As for the content of these questions, that is a problem that will depend for the most part on the particular case, and the ability of the individual *Defensor.* Suffice it to say that the preparation of these questions is actually one of the most important of the duties of the *Defensor.* Their effectiveness alone is sufficient to crown the work of the *Defensor* with success or failure. It is well also to keep in mind that the success of a *Defensor Vinculi* does not hinge upon the successful outcome of the cause for validity, but on the agreement of the final sentence of the court with objective truth.

The scope of this study has been limited to an examination of the rights and duties of the *Defensor Vinculi Matrimonialis,* a necessary official in every court that handles marriage cases. Regardless of the instance of the court to which the *Defensor* is attached, he is always ruled by the same law. Whether before the *Rota* or in the diocesan court of first instance, he is always obliged to appeal from the first sentence for nullity. Whether in first, third or fourth instance, he may never appeal from a sentence declaring a marriage to be valid.

The office is really a remarkable one. It is a most fitting monument to a Pope who was also a great canonist. Pope Benedict XIV saw a situation that called for a remedy, and he skillfully supplied the remedy—a remedy that Holy Mother Church has found so satisfactory, that she has retained it as a preventative.

APPENDIX I

The *Defensor Vinculi* in the Cases Ruled by Canon 1990

Canon 1990 enumerates a group of matrimonial cases which are exempted from the rigors of the solemn judicial process.[1]

This canon is also of some interest because it is the center of a dispute. It is disputed whether the process outlined in canons 1990, 1991 and 1992 is essentially judicial or administrative. Opinion is also divided as to whether the exemption of canon 1990 is to be limited to the cases mentioned in the canon, or extended to others of like nature. These questions are fully treated by many authors.[2]

These disputes in themselves are of little importance to the *Defensor Vinculi* except in the particular case in which he wishes to impugn the decision because of lack of competence arising from adherence to one or the other of these opinions.

The process outlined in the canon is informal, but the *Defensor Vinculi* must be cited as well as the parties. It would also seem that the *Defensor Vinculi* must actually be present at the hearing, inasmuch as the exception permitted by canon 1587, § 2, seems to be inoperative in these cases which are of a type that may be terminated in one hearing, and it is by no means certain that canon 1587, § 2, permits the *Defensor Vinculi* to be absent from all sessions of the hearing or trial.[3]

The *Defensor Vinculi* in this hearing, though the formalities of the regular trial are dispensed with, enjoys all the rights and duties that are his in any trial. He will act substantially in the same way that he would in the solemn trial.[4] In actual practice he

[1] *Cf.* Canon 1990.

[2] Kay, *Competence in Matrimonial Tribunals*, pp. 109-154; *Periodica de re morali, canonica, liturgica,* XX (1931), 93*-107*.

[3] "Si legitime citati aliquibus actibus . . . "—Canon 1587, § 2; *cf.* Chapter III of this study.

[4] Canons 1968 and 1969.

will have little need to exercise these rights to any great extent if the case truly falls under canon 1990.

One of his most important duties in these informal duties will be the examination and the study of the documents presented in the case. He must assure himself that the proof that they offer is certain, and not open to reasonable doubt.[5]

Since the process demands certainty he is obligated to insist that the impediment causing the nullification of the marriage be one of those listed in canon 1990 in conformity with the stricter opinion.[6] However, he may be overruled on this point, but the question is one which the judge must decide.

It is true that there is excellent reason to believe that the impediments are merely demonstratively listed in canon 1990, but the matter is not certain, and canon 1990 does demand certainty for the use of this abbreviated process. This insistency is clear from the wording of the canons of this group.[7]

The main differences between this informal hearing and the formal process are to be found in the nature of the appeal given from the decision of the judge and its consequences.

The *Defensor Vinculi* acting by virtue of canon 1990 is not obliged to appeal regardless of the merits of the case from the first decision for nullity. He is obliged to appeal only when he feels that the impediment claimed by the plaintiff is not certain, or that there is probability that a dispensation had been obtained.

In making this appeal, it must be clearly stated that the case was tried under the rules of canon 1990, 1991 and 1992.[8]

By the phrase *"non esse certa"* in canon 1991 is meant the absence of reasonable doubt.[9]

Reasonable probability that a dispensation was issued then is sufficient to oblige the *Defensor* to provoke the case to the next in-

[5] Noval, *De Processibus*, p. 580.

[6] Gasparri, *De Matrimonio*, II (1932 edit.), p. 307; Chelodi, *De Matrimonio*, p. 195; Fournet, *Le Mariage Chrétien*, p. 350.

[7] "Cum ex certo . . . "—Canon 1990; " . . . impedimenta de quibus in canon 1990 non esse certa . . . "—Canon 1991.

[8] ". . . scripto monendus est agi de casu excepto"—canon 1991.

[9] Noval, *De Processibus*, p. 580, n. 873.

stance if a decision for nullity has been received. In other words the absence of the dispensation must be equally as certain as the presence of the impediment causing the nullity of the marriage.

Another difference between the informal procedure and that of the solemn process is to be found in the manner in which the judge of the next instance reviews the case. This judge simply calls in his own *Defensor Vinculi* and with his assistance decides whether the decision of the lower instance is to be confirmed or rejected.[10]

Does the law permit the judge of the higher instance to confirm the decision of the lower court if the *Defensor Vinculi* disagrees?

In answering the question here raised it is well to bear in mind that the canon demands only the intervention of the *Defensor*. Of course when the *Defensor* is obliged to intervene he brings with him all his rights and duties. Canon 1992 further decrees that the case in second instance is to be handled in the same fashion as in first instance. It would seem, therefore, that if the *Defensor Vinculi* of the second instance were to disagree with the finding of the judge, he would enjoy the right of appealing to the next instance (the *Rota*) in the same manner that the case was appealed from first to second instance.

As for the practical aspect of the question, it would seem that the case under these circumstances should be sent back to the court of first instance for trial under the full form of the law. If the objections of the *Defensor Vinculi* were based on solid grounds, and were confirmed by the objections of the *Defensor* of the superior court, it would seem that the case in question could hardly have enjoyed the degree of certainty necessary to entitle it to the exemption of the documentary process.

As for the bare wording of the law, it requires the intervention of the *Defensor Vinculi* of the Curia during the review of the case by the higher tribunal, and seems to give to him in second instance, the same right he enjoys in first instance, that of provoking the case to a higher tribunal, when he believes such action to be neces-

[10] Canon 1992—"Iudex alterius instantiae, cum solo interventu defensoris vinculi, decernet. . . . "

sary.[11] This right is expressly given to the *Defensor Vinculi* of first instance by canon 1991, which is but a further explanation of canon 1990.

Another point of difference is found in the fact that if the appeal of the *Defensor Vinculi* is sustained by the higher instance, the case is then to be returned to the lower court for trial in the regular manner by the solemn process.[12]

One question remains that might cause difficulty in connection with the cases tried under the abbreviated process of canon 1990.

Shoud the *Defensor Vinculi* be mentioned in the decision closing one of these trials?

No specific rules are to be found in the law. However the intervention of the *Defensor Vinculi* is demanded under pain of nullifying the entire proceedings.[13]

Since the declaration of the nullity of a marriage is an act of great importance, the declaration should give the ordinary evidences that it is valid, hence, the presence of the *Defensor Vinculi*, a *sine qua non* for validity, should be indicated in the decision.

In conclusion it must be admitted that the trial held in accordance with canon 1990 is at least quasi-judicial in nature.[14] The *Defensor Vinculi* should therefore fulfill his duties in substantially the same manner as in the solemn trial, with the exception of the matter of appeals, since in this process appeal from the first decision for nullity is not mandatory.

[11] Canon 1992—". . . decernet eodem modo de quo in can. 1990. . . ."

[12] Canon 1992.

[13] Canon 1587, § 1.

[14] S. C. S. Off. (*Albanen. in America*), June 10, 1896—*Fontes*, n. 1180.

APPENDIX II

The *Defensor Vinculi* in the *Ratum et Non Consummatum* Process

This process, not a trial in the strict sense of the word, is purely an investigation, though a judicial one, for the purpose of certifying that conditions warrant the grant of a Papal Dispensation dissolving a nonconsummated marriage. In other words its purpose is simply and solely to gather evidence that will show the Sacred Congregation of the Sacraments that the marriage was not in fact consummated, and therefore enables the Congregation to assure His Holiness that he may safely grant the dispensation in the given case.[1]

The investigation is governed by the *Regulae Servandae* issued by the Sacred Congregation of the Sacraments on May 7, 1923 and the additional *Regulae* issued under the date of March 27, 1929.[2]

In general the investigation follows the same lines as the ordinary trial, omitting the pleadings, and all that follows the *conclusio in causa.*

Because of the fact that there is no summing up, no publication of the evidence (*publicatio processus*) and because the *Regulae Servandae* are more detailed than the Code, there will be some practical differences in the procedure worthy of separate discussion.

The duty of the *Defensor Vinculi* in these investigations is also somewhat different in principle. He does not contend that the marriage is valid, since the validity of the marriage is unquestioned. He is obliged, however, to attempt to prove by every legitimate means within his power that the marriage has been consummated.

The duty of the *Defensor Vinculi* to intervene in these cases derives from both the Code and the *Regulae Servandae* of the Sacred Congregation. The necessary intervention of the *Defensor Vinculi* in these cases is not an innovation of the Code of Canon Law, it is as old as the office itself, for Benedict XIV demanded that the *Defensor*

[1] *Reg. Serv. Super. Rato.*, n. 103; Lanier, *Guide Pratique,* p. 75, document XIV.

[2] *AAS,* XV (1923), 397 ff.; *AAS,* XXI (1929), 490 ff.

Vinculi intervene when the cause for proving nonconsummation of a marriage was tried at Rome.[3]

The *Regulae Servandae* of the Sacred Congregation in no place demand a radical departure from the ordinary law of the marriage trial, though in many places they are more detailed. In short special care and caution is demanded. Other differences arise from the purpose of this investigation which differentiates it from the ordinary trial concerned only with the question of the validity of the impugned marriage.

The rights and duties of the *Defensor Vinculi* are therefore substantially the same as in the ordinary trial excluding all that follows the *conclusio in causa.* Canons 1587, § 1, § 2, and 1968 and 1969 for example are quoted in the instruction practically verbatim, the differences arising solely from the nature of the *ratum et non consummatum* process. The canons are not merely quoted, they are also identified in the *Regulae* by number.[4]

It is therefore evident that the Sacred Congregation wishes these canons to be recognized as such, though slightly changed in the text of the *Regulae Servandae.* Accordingly the interpretation given to the *Regulae* should be in agreement with that given to their corresponding canons in the Code.

An example of the differences which must arise between the *Regulae* and similar canons of the Code is to be found in canon 1969, 4°, which gives a rule that could not possibly be applied in the *ratum et non consummatum* process. This canon declares that a motion of the *Defensor Vinculi* may be refused only by unanimous voice of the judges. Since only one judge presides over the *ratum et non consummatum* process, this provision is obviously inoperative. *Regula* 29, e, provides the substitute rule in the following words:

> Defensoris vinculi ius esto; . . . exigere ut alia acta, quae ipse suggesserit, conficiantur, nisi iudex dissentiat; quo in casu, si iudex non sit ipsemet Ordinarius, ad hunc recurrere fas est vinculi defensori.

[3] Benedict XIV, const., *Dei Miseratione,* November 3, 1741, n. 13—*Fontes,* n. 318.

[4] *Reg. Serv. Super. Rato.,* nn. 27, 28, 29.

The Ordinary is obviously the last resort in protest against a decree of the judge in this hearing. If the Ordinary himself presides over the trial, the *Defensor Vinculi* has no other remedy but to object to the denial in his final *Votum*. This situation is not as unfair as it would seem at first, for the Sacred Congregation ultimately gives the final decision on the matter and it is entirely free to ask for additional investigation if it feels that any phase of the trial has been incomplete.

In general therefore those *Regulae* which parallel canons of the Code, must be interpreted in the same manner as the canons themselves making allowance of course for those changes which of necessity arise from the actual wording of the *Regulae* due to the different purpose of this investigation.

Regula 27 may be cited in example. It is a paraphrase of canon 1587 adapted to suit this process. What has been said with regard to the presence of the *Defensor* in virtue of the law of canon 1587 will of necessity hold true of this *Regula*. Consequently it will also be doubtful that the *Defensor Vinculi* may be absent from all the sessions of the hearing, and yet insure the validity of the sessions by approving the *acta* after the sessions are closed. It is accordingly certain that he may be absent from some of the sessions and yet protect validity of these sessions by a later approval of the *acta*.[5]

In general, the law governing this process does not impose a radical department from the common law of the trial. The instruction, however, on several points being much more detailed frequently enforces the fulfillment of certain formalities that are no longer certainly required by the general law of the Code.

Despite the great essential similarity there are several points of difference that demand particular treatment.

The *Defensor Vinculi* in this process must be deputed by the Ordinary when he delegates the Curia to take care of the trial.[6] This appointment will of necessity have to be in writing and should be noted in the *acta* or minutes of the trial at the opening of the first session of the hearing.[7]

[5] *Reg. Serv. Super. Rato.*, n. 27, § 2.

[6] *Reg. Serv. Rato.*, n. 15; *cf.* canon 1589, § 1.

[7] *Reg. Serv. Super. Rato.*, nn. 15, 34, § 1, c.

The Ordinary may appoint as *Defensor Vinculi* either the *Defensor* of his Curia or another person properly fitted to fill the office if conditions warrant,[8] and always of course on the condition that he is not otherwise restricted in his delegation.

The *Defensor Vinculi* should not undertake to act in a case in which he is connected with either of the parties by reason of consanguinity, affinity or any other factor mentioned in canon 1613, § 1.[9]

The *Defensor Vinculi* is obliged to abstain from action on his own motion when he realizes he is liable to these exceptions.

If the judge acting for the Bishop in the case, discovers after the opening of the trial, that the *Defensor Vinculi* assigned by the Ordinary to the case is impeded from acting, then he, the judge, is empowered to elect a substitute *Defensor,* who also must have the qualifications required by the law. This substitute *Defensor Vinculi* must always be clearly designated in the *acta* or minutes as a substitute *Defensor.*[10]

This *Defensor Vinculi Substitutus* is to be distinguished from a *Defensor* specially chosen by the Ordinary at the beginning of the trial. This *Defensor* is not a *substitutus,* although he may not be the *Defensor Vinculi* permanently attached to the Curia.[11] The *Defensor Vinculi Substitutus* is always one who has been appointed after the opening of the trial to take the place of a regularly assigned *Defensor.*

Another difference between this hearing and the regular matrimonial trial is to be found in the requirement that the *Defensor Vinculi* is obliged to take the oath of office and secrecy every time he takes up a case.[12] In the ordinary formal matrimonial trial the permanently appointed *Defensor* is obliged to do so only when he takes up his office for the first time.[13]

The written assignment of the *Defensor Vinculi* to the case must

[8] *Reg. Serv. Super. Rato.,* n. 15.

[9] *Reg. Serv. Super. Rato.,* n. 16, §§ 1, 2.

[10] *Reg. Serv. Super. Rato.,* n. 18.

[11] *Reg. Serv. Super. Rato.,* nn. 13 and 15 in relation to n. 18.

[12] *Reg. Serv. Super. Rato.,* n. 19.

[13] Canon 1621, § 1.

be formally presented at the opening of the first session, at which time he must also take the oath of office and secrecy.[14]

In the event of the appointment of a *Defensor Vinculi Substitutus* the oath must be taken before he takes up his duties.

The rights of the *Defensor Vinculi* with regard to the calling of witnesses, and their examination, the examination of the parties, the reception of documentary proof are identical with those that he enjoys in the formal trial.

The very closest of parallels will be found to exist between *Regulae* 28 and 29 and canons 1968 and 1969.

The witnesses and parties are to be heard in the same manner as in the regular trial. The *Defensor Vinculi* supplies questions to be used by the judge in the examination. These questions prepared beforehand by the *Defensor Vinculi,* are delivered to the judge closed and sealed, and are opened in the act of examination itself. This is in entire conformity with the regular procedure for the examination of a witness in any matrimonial trial.

The questions in this trial as in the formal process, are of two kinds. The general questions destined to show the identity of the person being examined, and the special or particular questions destined to bring out the information possessed by the one undergoing examination. The instruction also warns that the questions should be short and brief, and not of a type known as leading questions.[15]

At the conclusion of the examination, the questions and answers recorded by the notary are read to the party or the witness, and after being acknowledged, they are signed first by the person who was examined, and then in turn by judge, *Defensor Vinculi* and notary.

The only departure from the ordinary procedure is the positive requirement of the instruction that the *Defensor* sign the testimony,[16] which is not to be found in the Code.[17]

The intervention of the *Defensor Vinculi* is positively required

[14] *Reg. Serv. Super Rato.*, nn. 19, 34, § 1, c. f.

[15] *Reg. Serv. Super. Rato.*, nn. 42, 43; canon 1774; Roberti, *De Processibus,* II, n. 347.

[16] *Reg. Serv. Super. Rato.*, n. 46.

[17] Canon 1780.

when the judge accepts or rejects witnesses called by the parties.[18] This gives the *Defensor Vinculi* an opportunity to oppose the admission of witness, when he believes such action is required to protect the interests of truth, as for instance in the event that the *Defensor* has reason to believe that the witness is untrustworthy.

The parties have also the right to request the reexamination of persons already examined, but the judge may permit this only by decree after having first consulted the *Defensor Vinculi* [19] and upon assurance that all danger of fraud is absent.

Whenever the Ordinary himself is not presiding, the *Defensor Vinculi* will always enjoy the right to have recourse to him against the refusal of any of his motions by the delegated judge.[20]

This is the only road of action open to the *Defensor,* but if defeated it must be remembered that he can mention the fact in his *Votum,* then the final decision will rest with the Sacred Congregation, for in the last analysis it must make the final decision on whether the process has produced sufficient certainty of nonconsummation to justify them in recommending the case to the Holy Father.

The obligation imposed on the judge *instructor* to hear the *Defensor Vinculi* by no means obliges him to follow the recommendations of the *Defensor.* He is bound only to give reasonable consideration to the arguments of the *Defensor* and, since it is the judge *instructor* who is the moderator of the hearing, and the one charged with its direction, he has the deciding voice in all questions that may arise, saving recourse by parties or *Defensor* to the Ordinary.

Before leaving the general treatment of the examination of parties and witnesses, to proceed to special phases of the law, it is well to take notice of one general principle that governs the hearing whenever questions are answered before the court. It is found in *Regula* 31, which states, that both the judge *instructor* and the *Defensor Vinculi* have a common obligation to see that the questions put to the witnesses and parties are fully and properly answered.

At times it will be found that either one of the parties or some of

[18] *Reg. Serv. Super. Rato.,* n. 22, § 1.

[19] *Reg. Serv. Super. Rato.,* n. 47, §§ 1, 2, 3; 22.

[20] *Reg. Serv. Super. Rato.,* n. 29, c.; note: n. 22, § 2, gives the same right to the parties.

the witnesses live at some distance from the place of the hearing. They may live either in a distant part of the same diocese or in another diocese. These people can hardly be expected to appear at the cost of considerable trouble and expense at the place of the hearing itself.

Regula 23 of this instruction provides that if one of the witnesses is found to dwell in another diocese, the judge *instructor* is to request the Ordinary of that place to call the witness before his own tribunal, and there to examine the witness with the prepared questions of the *Defensor Vinculi.* The Ordinary will then return the results of the examination conducted by himself or his delegate according to the prescriptions of the law, to the judge who is hearing the case.[21]

The procedure outlined in the instruction is very similar to that prescribed by the Code for the formal process in canon 1770, § 2, 3°, 4°. The same difficulties concerning the participation of the *Defensor Vinculi* in the execution of rogatory commissions present themselves.

Regulae 23 and 24 which regulate these proceedings under the instruction are, however, a little more detailed than canon 1770.

That the *Defensor* is obliged to prepare the questions to be used by the commissioned judge is certain, but should the judge acting by virtue of a rogatory commission call in the *Defensor* attached to his own Curia to assist at the examination?

Consideration of *Regulae* 23 and 24 would seem to indicate that he should do so. The questions used are, of course, those prepared by the *Defensor Vinculi* appointed to the case by the Bishop of the place of the hearing, but it must be remembered that the right of the *Defensor Vinculi* to interject *ex officio* questions during the progress of the examination of a witness or party, constitutes a very important phase of his duties.

It is well also to bear in mind that, if the person were being examined at the place of the trial itself, both judge and *Defensor* would be enjoined to protect the perpetuity of consummated marriage.[22] Is

[21] *Reg. Serv. Super Rato.*, 23, canons 1570, § 2; 1770, § 2, 3°.

[22] Both the judge *instructor* and the *Defensor Vinculi* have the joint obligation to see that the questions are fully and properly answered; *cf. Reg. Serv. Super. Rato.*, n. 31.

it likely that the law intends to omit this extra safeguard when a witness or a party is being examined by a judge who is under the additional handicap of being unfamiliar with the particular case involved in the trial?

An examination of the similar case in which a witness is to be heard who dwells in a distant part of the same diocese discloses that the instruction is explicit in demanding the presence of someone as a substitute *Defensor Vinculi* unless it is impossible to find a priest to fill the position.[23]

A closer examination of the *Regulae* seems to justify the conclusion that the *Defensor Vinculi* of the Curia should also be called to assist at the examination of a witness for another court. According to the *Regulae,* the Ordinary of the place where the person to be examined is now located, is obliged to see that the sessions of the examination follow all the prescriptions of the law:

> Ordinarius hac de re requisitus, iuris servatis praescriptionibus, acta per se vel per alium confecta, ad iudicem remittat.[24]

Since the presence of the *Defensor Vinculi* is required in all sessions of these trials,[25] it is only logical to conclude that the presence of the *Defensor Vinculi* of the Curia is also mandatory whenever the court acts by virtue of a rogatory commission arising from the *ratum et non consummatum* process.

The *Defensor Vinculi* thus assisting at the hearing of a witness for another court, would be obliged to take the oath of office and secrecy before he could take part in the hearing.[26]

The "Septimae Manus" Witnesses

The *Septimae Manus* witnesses are witnesses called to vouch for the credibility of the parties and thus give support to their claims.[27] They are examined in the customary way with the questions of the

[23] *Reg. Serv. Super. Rato.,* n. 22, §§ 2, 4.

[24] *Reg. Serv. Super. Rato.,* n. 23.

[25] *Reg. Serv. Super. Rato.,* n. 27, § 2.

[26] *Reg. Serv. Super. Rato.,* nn. 19, 24, § 3.

[27] *Reg. Serv. Super. Rato.,* n. 60, § 1; Lanier, *Guide Pratique,* p. 41.

Defensor Vinculi,[28] but the questions must be contrived so as to indicate that these witnesses attest principally to the credibility of the spouse on whose behalf they were called.

Whenever possible each of the parties should call seven of these witnesses, though where this is impossible a lesser number is acceptable. The reason for the smaller number should always be indicated in the *acta*.[29]

The *Septimae Manus* witnesses may also have actual knowledge of the fact of nonconsummation, in which event they should be properly questioned in connection with this knowledge in the fashion of other witnesses.[30]

They are questioned first with the questions of the *Defensor Vinculi*, and then with the questions proposed by the parties. At the end of the questioning, both questions and answers are read to the witness for his or her approval. This done, the witness should sign the testimony, followed in turn by judge, *Defensor Vinculi* and notary.[31]

The Physical Examination

The *Defensor Vinculi* has the same duties in connection with this proof under *ratum et non consummatum* process that he has in the like examination prescribed by the Code.[32]

While the Code does not demand the *balneus tepidus*, the *Regulae Servandae* do so, except under circumstances in which the doctors declare it to be either useless or harmful.[33]

The details of the law do not directly concern the *Defensor Vinculi*, except in so far as he is obliged to insist on the full observance of the *Regulae Servandae*. The procedure follows along the same lines as the Code in connection with the submission of the doctors' reports and the consequent examination of the physicians with the questions of the *Defensor Vinculi*.[34]

[28] Lanier, *Guide Pratique*, pp. 40, 71.

[29] *Reg. Serv. Super. Rato.*, n. 59.

[30] *Reg. Serv. Super. Rato.*, 60, § 2.

[31] *Reg. Serv. Super. Rato.*, n. 69.

[32] *Cf.* canons 1976-1981.

[33] *Reg. Serv. Super. Rato.*, n. 92.

[34] *Cf. Reg. Serv. Super. Rato.*, n. 93 and canon 1981.

The *Defensor Vinculi* should be specially vigilant in connection with the physical examination to guard against the fraudulent substitution of one person for another. Consequently he should take special care to see that the precautions demanded by the recent instruction of 1929 are observed.[35]

The medical experts are of course chosen by the court in consultation with the *Defensor Vinculi*,[36] who is always bound to see that these specialists really enjoy the reputations that they lay claim to. In practice this duty will be insignificant because the qualifications of the doctors and other experts will generally be decided beforehand.

The Close of the Hearing

This trial cannot be brought to a close until the *Defensor Vinculi* has indicated that he has rested his case.[37]

Before the judge may issue the decree closing the case, both he and the *Defensor Vinculi* must separately study the *acta* of the case, in order to assure themselves that the aforesaid *acta* are complete.[38]

Since there is neither publication of the process (*publicatio processus*), nor summing up (*discussio causae*) in these hearings, the next step will be the writing of the opinions of the *Defensor Vinculi* and the Ordinary.

The *Defensor Vinculi* will have the *acta* or the minutes of the investigation completely at his disposal during the writing of his *Votum*.[39]

With the writing of these opinions the hearing closes, and once these opinions or *vota*, have been received, the entire case is sent to the Sacred Congregation of the Sacraments.[40]

The *Defensor Vinculi* in the writing of his *Votum*, should note especially the observance of the nonobservance of the *Regulae Servandae* of the Sacred Congregation of the Sacraments, as well as the

[35] Instr., S. C. de Sacram., March 27, 1929—*AAS*, XXI (1929), p. 490.

[36] *Reg. Serv. Super. Rato.*, n. 87.

[37] *Reg. Serv. Super. Rato.*, n. 96, § 1.

[38] *Reg. Serv. Super. Rato.*, n. 96, §§ 2, 3.

[39] *Reg. Serv. Super. Rato.*, n. 98, § 1; A Coronata, *De Processibus*, p. 433, n. 1497.

[40] *Reg. Serv. Super. Rato.*, n. 98, § 1.

additional *Normae* of March 27, 1929 for the prevention of the fraudulent substitution of one person for another.[41]

When writing the opinion, the *Defensor Vinculi* should not adhere to the plaintiff unless the case is an evident one.[42] He should therefore strive to raise every legitimate objection to the arguments for the nonconsummation of the marriage. These objections of course should be real objections, not mere sophistries.

Concluding Remarks

The general rule of procedure in this type of trial requires the judge *instructor* to accept or reject all motions of the parties by decree having first consulted the *Defensor Vinculi.*[43]

In some of the transactions of the process the *Regulae* explicitly demand the procedure to follow this form. The judge for instance decides by decree on the admission or rejection of witnesses and proofs,[44] the selection of translators,[45] the recall of witnesses,[46] but in every case he must have consulted the *Defensor Vinculi.*

These are instances in which the *Regulae Servandae* specifically demand the aforementioned judicial matters to be terminated by decree of the court after consultation with the *Defensor Vinculi.* This procedure would have to be followed even if the *Regulae Servandae* did not demand it in the particular case because *Regula* 22, § 1, imposes it on the whole process, making it a general rule. Thus for instance while there is no specific *Regula* requiring that interpreters should be selected in this manner, yet when necessary, they too should be selected by decree of the judge after he has heard both parties and *Defensor Vinculi.*

There is a remedy against this decree of the judge only when the trial is presided over by a judge *instructor,* against whom recourse may be had to the Ordinary. If the Ordinary himself presides over the hearing, which will seldom happen, the *Defensor Vinculi* has no

[41] *AAS,* XXI (1929), 490; A Coronata, *De Processibus,* p. 433, n. 1497.

[42] Sipos, *Enchiridion,* p. 833.

[43] *Reg. Serv. Super. Rato.,* n. 22, § 1.

[44] *Reg. Serv. Super. Rato.,* n. 22, § 1.

[45] *Reg. Serv. Super. Rato.,* n. 49.

[46] *Reg. Serv. Super. Rato.,* n. 56, §§ 1, 3.

means to oppose the decree other than to attack it in his final *Votum.*

In all the instances in which the *Defensor Vinculi* must be heard, he should not act in an arbitrary manner, neither should he oppose the admission of witnesses or proofs, simply because facts prejudicial to his side of the case may be revealed. The *Defensor Vinculi* should always be motivated by a desire to disclose the truth, rather than to blindly urge his own cause. He should therefore oppose the motions of the parties, only when he fears that they will result in the presentation of untrustworthy witnesses or evidence, as might be the case when he has good reason to believe that a witness is not worthy of credibility, or that a document is doubtful either in its application to the case or in its authenticity.

One of the outstanding characteristics of the *ratum et non consummatum* process is its lack of both *publicatio processus* and *discussio causae.* Because of this limitation, the parties at times may find it very necessary to petition the judge to disclose to them the names of the witnesses appearing against them.

The judge may permit this by decree after having heard the *Defensor Vinculi,* but he should not do so until after the witnesses have been heard.[47]

It is quite evident after but a brief study of the *Regulae Servandae* of the *ratum et non consummatum* process, that while the investigation is regulated by certain general rules, the *Regulae Servandae* in many places make specific application of the general rule to the particular incident of the hearing. This is merely an evidence of the thoroughness with which these *Regulae* have been drawn up.

Also evident will be the fact that the underlying legal principles of the process are the same as those given in the Code for the solemn matrimonial process and the trial in general. Differences, of course do occur, but it will be found that the chief characteristic of the *Regulae Servandae* rests in their completeness and thoroughness, rather than in any difference distinguishing this process from the ordinary canonical trial. The importance of the issue at stake, the sacred character of the sacrament of Matrimony and its spiritual consequences for the parties involved, amply justify the more than painstaking care with which these *Regulae* were composed.

[47] *Reg. Serv. Super. Rato.,* nn. 63, 1, 2.

BIBLIOGRAPHY

Sources

Acta Apostolicae Sedis (AAS), Romae, 1909.

Acta Sanctae Sedis (AAS), 41 vols., Romae, 1865-1908.

Canones et Decreta Concilii Tridentini, 19 ed., Taurini, 1913.

Codex Iuris Canonici Pii X Pontificis Maximi iussu digestu Benedicti Papae XV auctoritate promulgatus, Romae, 1918.

Codex Juris Canonici Fontes, 6 vols., Romae, 1923-1932.

Collectanea Sacrae Congregationis de Propaganda Fide, 2 vols., Romae, 1907.

Collectio Lacensis, Acta et Decreta Sacrorum Conciliorum Recentiorum (Coll. Lacen.), 7 vols., Friburgi Br., 1870-1890.

Concilii Plenarii Baltimorensis III, *Acta et Secreta,* Baltimorensi, 1886.

Corpus Iuris Canonici, Editio Lipsiensis II, 2 vols., Lipsiae, 1922.

Corpus Iuris Civilis, 3 vols., Berolini, 1928-1829.

Hardouin, *Conciliorum Collectio Regia Maxima,* 12 vols., Parisiis, 1715.

Migne, *Patrologia Graeca* (MPG), 161 vols., Parisiis, 1858-1864.

Regulae Servandae in Iudiciis apud S. Romanae Rotae Tribunal (Regulae S. R. Rotae), Romae, 1910.

Sanctae Romanae Rotae Decisiones seu Sententiae, Romae, 1912.

Works of Reference

Ayrinhac, Henry A., *General Legislation in the New Code of Canon Law,* New York, 1923.

Albers, P. S.J., *Enchiridion Historiae Ecclesiasticae,* 3 vols., Neomagi in Hollandia, 1910.

(Bachofen), Charles Augustine, *A Commentary on the New Code of Canon Law,* 8 vols., St. Louis, 1918-1922.

Benedictus XIV, *De Synodo Dioecesana,* 2 vols., Romae, 1806.

Benedictus XIV, *De Servorum Dei Beatificatione et Beatorum Canonizatione,* Bologna, 1734.

Benedictus XIV, *Opera Omnia,* 17 vols., Prati, 1839-1847.

Benedictus XIV, *Quaestiones Canonicae et Morales,* Prati, 1844.

Bouix, *De Judiciis Ecclesiasticis,* 3d ed., 2 vols., Parisiis, 1884.

Bouuaert, F. C., Simenon, G., *Manuale Juris Canonici,* 2d ed., Bandae et Leodii, 1926.

Campagna, Angelo, *Il Vicario Generale del Vescovo,* Washington, D. C., 1931.

Cance, Adrien, *Le Code de Droit Canonique,* 3 vols., Parisiis, 1929.

Cappello, Felix M., *Tractatus Canonico Moralis de Sacramentis,* 3 vols., Romae, 1926-1928.

Cappello, Felix M., *Summa Iuris Publici Ecclesiastici*, Romae, 1928.
Catholic Encyclopedia, The, 16 vols., New York, 1912.
Chelodi, Joannes, *Jus Matrimoniale*, 3d ed., Tridenti, 1921.
Chelodi, Joannes, *Jus de Personis*, 2d ed., Tridenti, 1927.
Cicognani, Hamletus J., *Commentarium ad Librum I Codicis*, 2 vols., Romae, 1925.
Cocchi, Guidus, *Commentarium in Codicem Juris Canonici ad usum Scholarum*, 8 vols., Taurinorum Augustae, 1925-1928.
Connolly, T. A., *Appeals*, Washington, D. C., 1932.
Coronata, Matheus a, *Institutiones Juris Canonici*, 2 vols., Taurini, 1928.
De Becker, Julius, *De Sponsalibus et Matrimonio Praelectiones Canonicae*, Bruxellis, 1896.
De Becker, Julius, *De Matrimonio*, Lovanii, 1931.
De Justis, Vincentius, *De Dispensationibus Matrimonialibus*, Lucae, 1726.
Dictionaire de Droit Canonique, 2 vols., Parisiis, 1844.
Dugan, Henry Francis, *The Judiciary Department of the Dioecesan Curia*, Washington, D. C., 1925.
Durandus, Guillielmus, *Speculum Juris*, 3 vols., Venettiis, 1577.
Encyclopédie Théologique, 50 vols., Paris, 1844.
Esmein, A., *Le Mariage en Droit Canonique*, 2 vols., Parissis, 1891.
Farrugia, Nicholaus, *De Matrimonio et Causis Matrimonialibus*, Taurini, 1924.
Feije, Henricus Joannes, *De Impedimentis et Dispensationibus Matrimonialibus*, Lovanii, 1874.
Fourneret, Pierre, *Le Mariage Chrétien*, Parisiis, 1925.
Gasparri, Petrus, *Tractatus Canonicus de Matrimonio*, 2 vols., Parisiis, 1891.
Gasparri, Petrus, *Tractus Canonicus de Matrimonio*, 2 vols., Romae, 1932.
Gougnard, A., *Tractatus de Matrimonio*, 7th ed., Mechliniae, 1931.
Grandclaude, E., *Jus Canonicum juxta Ordinem Decretalium*, 3 vols., Parisiis, 1883.
Hostiensis, Henricus Cardinalis, *Summa Aurea*, Lugduni, 1586.
Joyce, George Hayward, S.J., *Christian Marriage*, London, 1933.
Kay, Thomas, *Competence in Matrimonial Procedure*, Washington, D. C., 1929.
Lanier, C. Henri, *Guide Pratique de la Procédure Matrimoniale en Droit Canonique*, Parisiis, 1927.
Laurentius, Josephus, S.J., *Institutiones Juris Ecclesiastici*, Friburgi, Br., 1903.
Lega, Michael, *De Judiciis Ecclesiasticis*, 2 vols., Romae, 1896.
Linneborn, Johannes, *Grundriss des Eherechts*, Paderborn, 1922.
Mansella, Josephus, *De Impedimentibus Matrimonium Dirimentibus ac de Processu Judiciali in Causis Matrimonialibus*, Romac, 1881.
Muñiz, T., *Procedimientos Eclesiásticos*, 3 vols., Seville, 1930.
Noval, Josephus, *De Judiciis*, Romae, 1920.
Ojetti B., *Commentarium in Codicem Juris Canonici*, 2 vols., Romae, 1931.
Payen, G., *De Matrimonio in Missionibus*, 3 vols., Zi-Ka-Wei, 1928-1929.
Pellegrini, Carolus, *Praxis Vicariorum*, Venetiis, 1706.

Peries, G., *Code de Procédure Canonique dans les Causes Matrimoniales,* Parisiis, 1894.
Reiffenstuel, Anacletus, *Jus Canonicum Universum,* 4 vols., Venetiis, 1735.
Roberti, Franciscus, *De Processibus,* 2 vols., Romae, 1926.
Santi, Franciscus, *Praelectiones Juris Canonici,* 4 vols., Ratisbonae, 1886.
Schmalzgrueber, F., *Jus Ecclesiasticum Universum,* 12 vols., Romae, 1845.
Sipos, Stephanus, *Enchiridion Juris Canonici, Pécs,* 1926.
Smith, S. B., *Elements of Ecclesiastical Law,* 2 vols., New York, 1883.
Smith, S. B., *The Marriage Process in the United States,* New York, 1893.
Sperelli, *Decisiones Fori Ecclesiastici,* 2 vols., Venetiis, 1666.
Vermeersch, A.-Creusen, J., *Epitome Juris Canonici,* 3 vols., 1927.
Wernz, Franciscus, *Jus Decretalium,* 6 vols., Romae, 1906-1913.
Wernz, F.-Vidal, P., *Jus Canonicum,* 4 vols., Romae, 1927-1928.

PERIODICALS

Apollinaris, Commentarium Juridico-Canonicum, Romae, 1928.
Archiv fur Katholisches Kirchenrecht (AKKR), Mainz, 1857.
Irish Ecclesiastical Record, The (IER), Dublin, 1864.
Jus Pontificium, Romae, 1921.
Theologisch-praktische Quartalschrift (*Th. Pr. QS*), Linz, 1832.
Periodica de Re Morali, Canonica, Liturgica, Romae et Brugis, 1912.

UNIVERSITAS CATHOLICA AMERICAE

WASHINGTON, D. C.

FACULTAS JURIS CANONICI

No. 85

1934

ALPHABETICAL INDEX

Abbots Nullius, their power to appoint a *Defensor Vinculi*, 17.

Accessus Judicialis, 80.

Acta, right of the *Defensor Vinculi* to inspect, 44.

Administrator Apostolic, his power to appoint a *Densor Vinculi*, 17; may remove him, 27.

Appointment of the *Defensor Vinculi*, 17; must be in writing, 23.

Appeal, Judicial, 99; obligation of the *Defensor Vinculi* to appeal, 100, 101, 102, 103, 104, 110, 114, 121, 124; meaning of the term "two conformable sentences," 116.

Benedict XIV, ix, 1, 13.

Calling of witnesses, 56.

Canon 1990, 126, 127, 128, 129.

"Catholica Doctrina," xii, 75, 130.

Complaint of Nullity, 99, 119, 120.

Concordantia Dubiorum, 57.

Conclusio in Causa, 84, 85.

Conditions that moved Pope Benedict XIV to establish the office of *Defensor Vinculi*, 14.

Contempt, The Declaration of, 77.

Contumacy, The Declaration of, 77.

Defensores in Roman Law, 1.

"Dei Miseratione," ix, x, 29, 42, 111.

Discussio Causae, 86.

Documents entered in the trial, 78.

Documentary Process, The, 126, 127, 128, 129.

Excommunication, its effects, 26.

Experts, 71.

Final Sentence, The, 91; its drafting by the collegiate tribunal, 92.

Fiscus, 9.

Incidental Trial, The, 93, 94, 95, 96, 97.

Instruction of the S. C. C., August 22, 1840, xi, 42, 68, 75.

Instruction of the S. C. S. Officii (*ad Ep. Rituum Orient.*) a. 1883, xi, 43, 68, 75.

Interpreters, 80.

Interrogatories of the *Defensor*, 57, 63, 64, 67, 125, 134.

Intervention required of the *Defensor Vinculi*, 35, 38, 39, 40.

Libellus, The Introductory, 46, 48; recourse against its rejection, 50.

Loss of Office by the *Defensor*, 26.

Oath of office, 33.

Oath, Suppletory, 79.

Ocular Inspection, 80.

Officialis, his lack of power to appoint a *Defensor*, 19; his power to punish a negligent *Defensor*, 23; to remove him if necessary, 24.

Origin of the Office of *Defensor Vinculi*, 1; the suggestion of Hostiensis, 5; derived from the Promotor of Justice, 9; a *praxis* recognized by the S. C. C., 10.

Periti, 71.

Physical Examination, The, 138.

Plurality of offices, same person may be Promotor of Justice and *Defensor Vinculi* if the work is not too great, 32; Vicar General should not be *Defensor Vinculi*, 32.

Pre-Benedictine Defense of the Marriage Bond, 2.

Prefects Apostolic, their power to appoint a *Defensor Vinculi*, 17.

Prelates, Nullius, their power to appoint a *Defensor Vinculi*, 17.

Preliminary acts that must be placed by the *Defensor Vinculi*, 33.

Presence required of the *Defensor Vinculi* in the trial, 36, 41, 64.
Pro-Vicars and Pro-Prefects, their lack of power to appoint a *Defensor Vinculi*, 17.
Profession of Faith, The, 34.
Prohibition of the exercise of rights, 82.
Promotor Fidei, 13.
Promotor of Justice, 9.
Publicatio Processus, 84.
Qualifications that the *Defensor* should possess, 28, 29.
Quasi-domcile, the preliminary investigation that is required when the competence of the court is derived from this title, 50, 53.
Querela Nullitatis, 99, 119, 120.
Questions of the *Defensor Vinculi*, 57, 63, 64, 67, 125, 134.
Ratum et non consummatum process, 130, 131, 132, 133, 134, 137, 138, 139.
Remedies against the final sentence, 99.
Removal of the *Defensor Vinculi* by the Bishop, 25; by the *Officialis*, 24; by the Vicar General, 26.
Residential Bishops, their power to appoint a *Defensor Vinculi*, 17.
Restitutio in integrum, 99.
Rogatory Commissions, 73; the *Defensor* who supplies the questions, 74; required presence of the *Defensor* of the assisting Curia, 75.
Septimae Manus Witnesses, 137.
Sequestration, 82.
Summing Up, The, 86.
Suppletory Oath, The, 79.
Suspension, its effects, 26.
Suspicion, the exception of, 29.
Tenure of office of the *Defensor Vinculi*, 25.
Vicar Apostolic, his power to appoint a *Defensor Vinculi*, 17.
Vicar Capitular, his power over the *Defensor Vinculi*, 22, 27.
Vicar Delegate, his lack of power to appoint a *Defensor Vinculi*, 18.
Vicar General, his power to appoint a *Defensor Vinculi*, 17, 18, 32.
Witnesses, Their Examination, 58, 60, 61, 63, 64, 66, 67, 125, 134.

Vita

John Leo Dolan was born on April 19, 1906, in New York City. He received his elementary education in the parochial school of St. Charles Borromeo, and his high school and college training in Cathedral College, New York City. He pursued his theological studies at St. Joseph's Seminary, Dunwoodie, New York. He was ordained priest on September 19, 1931, and in the same year entered the School of Canon Law at the Catholic University of America, in Washington, D. C.

CANON LAW STUDIES

1. Freriks, Rev. Celestine A., C.PP.S., J.C.D., Religious Congregations in Their External Relations, 121 pp., 1916.
2. Galliher, Rev. Daniel M., O.P., J.C.D., Canonical Elections, 117 pp., 1917.
3. Borkowski, Rev. Aurelius L., O.F.M., De Confraternitatibus Ecclesiasticis, 136 pp., 1918.
4. Castillo, Rev. Cayo, J.C.D., Disertacion Historico-canonica sobre la Potestad del Cabildo en Sede Vacante o Impedida del Vicario Capitular, 99 pp., 1919 (1918).
5. Kubelbeck, Rev. William J., S.T.B., J.C.D., The Sacred Penitentiaria and Its Relations to Faculties of Ordinaries and Priests, 129 pp., 1918.
6. Petrovits, Rev. Joseph J. C., S.T.D., J.C.D., The New Church Law on Matrimony, X-461 pp., 1919.
7. Hickey, Rev. John J., S.T.B., J.C.D., Irregularities and Simple Impediments in the New Code of Canon Law, 100 pp., 1920.
8. Klekotka, Rev. Peter J., S.T.B., J.C.D., Diocesan Consultors, 179 pp., 1920.
9. Wannenmacher, Rev. Francis, J.C.D., The Evidence in Ecclesiastical Procedure Affecting the Marriage Bond, 1920. (Not Printed.)
10. Golden, Rev. Henry Francis, J.C.D., Parochial Benefices in the New Code, IV-119 pp., 1921. (Printed 1925.)
11. Koudelka, Rev. Charles, J., J.C.D., Pastors, Their Rights and Duties According to the New Code of Canon Law, 211 pp., 1921.
12. Melo, Rev. Antonius, O.F.M., J.C.D., De Exemptione Regularium, X-188 pp., 1921.
13. Schaaf, Rev. Valentine Theodore, O.F.M., S.T.B., J.C.D., The Cloister, X-180 pp., 1921.
14. Burke, Rev. Thomas Joseph, S.T.B., J.C.D., Competence in Ecclesiastical Tribunals, IV-117 pp., 1922.
15. Leech, Rev. George Leo, J.C.D., A Comparative Study of the Constitution "Apostolicae Sedis" and the "Codex Juris Canonici," 179 pp., 1922.
16. Motry, Rev. Hubert Louis, S.T.D., J.C.D., Diocesan Faculties According to the Code of Canon Law, II-167 pp., 1922.
17. Murphy, Rev. George Lawrence, J.C.D., Delinquencies and Penalties in the Administration and the Reception of the Sacraments, IV-121 pp., 1923.
18. O'Reilly, Rev. John Anthony, S.T.B., J.C.D., Ecclesiastical Sepulture in the New Code of Canon Law, II-129 pp., 1923.
19. Michalicka, Rev. Wenceslas Cyrill, O.S.B., J.C.D., Judicial Procedure in Dismissal of Clerical Exempt Religious, 107 pp., 1923.

20. DARGIN, REV. EDWARD VINCENT, S.T.B., J.C.D., Reserved Cases According to the Code of Canon Law, IV-103 pp., 1924.
21. GODFREY, REV. JOHN A., S.T.B., J.C.D., The Right of Patronage According to the Code of Canon Law, 153 pp., 1924.
22 HAGEDORN, REV. FRANCIS EDWARD, J.C.D., General Legislation on Indulgences, II-154 pp., 1924.
23. KING, REV. JAMES IGNATIUS, J.C.D., The Administration of the Sacraments to Dying Non-Catholics, V-141 pp., 1924.
24. WINSLOW, REV. FRANCIS JOSEPH, A.F.M., J.C.D., Vicars and Prefects Apostolic, IV-149 pp., 1924.
25. CORREA, REV. JOSE SERVELION, S.T.L., J.C.D., La Potestad Legislativa de la Iglesia Católica, IV-127 pp., 1925.
26. DUGAN, REV. HENRY FRANCIS, M.A., J.C.D., The Judiciary Department of the Diocesan Curia, 87 pp., 1925.
27. KELLER, REV. CHARLES FREDERICK, S.T.B., J.C.D., Mass Stipends, 167 pp., 1925.
28. PASCHANG, REV. JOHN LINUS, J.C.D., The Sacramentals According to the Code of Canon Law, 129 pp., 1925.
29. PIONTEK, REV. CYRILLUS, O.F.M., S.T.B., J.C.D., De Indulto Exclaustrationis necnon Saecularizationis, XIII-289 pp., 1925.
30. KEARNEY, REV. RICHARD JOSEPH, S.T.B., J.C.D., Sponsors at Baptism According to the Code of Canon Law, IV-127 pp., 1925.
31. BARTLETT, REV. CHESTER JOSEPH, A.M., LL.B., J.C.D., The Tenure of Parochial Property in the United States of America, V-108 pp., 1926.
32. KILKER, REV. ADRIAN JEROME, J.C.D., Extreme Unction, V-425 pp. 1926.
33. MCCORMICK, REV. ROBERT EMMETT, J.C.D., Confessors of Religious, VIII-266 pp., 1926.
34. MILLER, REV. NEWTON THOMAS, J.C.D., Founded Masses According to the Code of Canon Law, VII-93 pp., 1926.
35. ROELKER, REV. EDWARD G., S.T.D., J.C.D., Principles of Privilege According to the Code of Canon Law, XI-166 pp., 1926.
36. BAKALARCZYK, REV. RICHARDUS, M.I.C., J.U.D., De Novitiatu, VIII-208 pp., 1927.
37. PIZZUTI, REV. LAWRENCE, O.F.M., J.U.L., De Parochis Religiosis, 1927. (Not Printed.)
38. BLILEY, REV. NICHOLAS MARTIN, O.S.B., J.C.D., Altars According to the Code of Canon Law, XIX-132 pp., 1927.
39. BROWN, BRENDAN FRANCIS, A.B., LL.M., J.U.D., The Canonical Juristic Personality with Special Reference to its Status in the United States of America, V-212 pp., 1927.
40. CAVANAUGH, REV. WILLIAM THOMAS, C.P., J.U.D., The Reservation of the Blessed Sacrament, VIII-101 pp., 1927.
41. DOHENY, REV. WILLIAM J., C.S.C., A.B., J.U.D., Church Property: Modes of Acquisition, X-118 pp,. 1927

42. Feldhaus, Rev. Aloysius H., C.PP.S., J.C.D., Oratories, IX-141 pp., 1927.
43. Kelly, Rev. James Patrick, A.B., J.C.D., The Jurisdiction of the Simple Confessor, X-208 pp., 1927.
44. Neuberger, Rev. Nicholas J., J.C.D., Canon 6 or the Relation of the Codex Juris Canonici to the Preceding Legislation, V-95 pp., 1927.
45. O'Keeffe, Rev. Gerald Michael, J.C.D., Matrimonial Dispensations, Powers of Bishops, Priests, and Confessors, VIII-232 pp., 1927.
46. Quigley, Rev. Joseph, A.M., A.B., J.C.D., Condemned Societies, 139 pp., 1927.
47. Zaplotnik, Rev. Ioannes Leo, J.C.D., De Vicariis Foraneis, X-142 pp., 1927.
48. Duskie, Rev. John Aloysius, A.B., J.C.D., The Canonical Status of the Orientals in the United States, VIII-196 pp., 1928.
49. Hyland, Rev. Francis Edward, J.C.D., Excommunication, Its Nature, Historical Development and Effects, VIII-181 pp., 1928.
50. Reinmann, Rev. Gerald Joseph, O.M.C., J.C.D., The Third Order Secular of Saint Francis, 201 pp., 1928.
51. Schenk, Rev. Francis J., J.C.D., The Matrimonial Impediments of Mixed Religion and Disparity of Cult, XVI-318 pp., 1929.
52. Coady, Rev. John Joseph, S.T.D., J.U.D., A.M., The Appointment of Pastors, VIII-150 pp., 1929.
53. Kay, Rev. Thomas Henry, J.C.D., Competence in Matrimonial Procedure, VIII-164 pp., 1929.
54. Turner, Rev. Sidney Joseph, C.P., J.U.D., The Vow of Poverty, XLIX-217 pp., 1929.
55. Kearney, Rev. Raymond A., A.B., S.T.D., J.C.D., The Principles of Delegation, VII-149 pp., 1929.
56. Conran, Rev. Edward James, A.B., J.C.D., The Interdict, V-163 pp., 1930.
57. O'Neil, Rev. William H., J.C.D., Papal Rescripts of Favor, VII-218 pp., 1930.
58. Bastnagel, Rev. Clement Vincent, J.U.D., The Appointment of Parochial Adjutants and Assistants, XV-257 pp., 1930.
59. Ferry, Rev. William A., A.B., J.C.D., Stole Fees, X-107 pp., 1930.
60. Costello, Rev. John Michael, A.B., J.C.D., Domicile and Quasi-Domicile, VII-201 pp., 1930.
61. Kremer, Rev. Michael Nicholas, A.B., S.T.B., J.C.D., Church Support in the United States, VI-136 pp., 1930.
62. Angulo, Rev. Luis, C.M., J.C.D., Legislación de la Iglesia sobre la intención en la applicación de la Santa Misa, VII-104 pp., 1931.
63. Frey, Rev. Wolfgang Norbert, O.S.B., A.B., J.C.D., The Act of Religious Profession, VIII-174 pp., 1931.
64. Roberts, Rev. James Brendan, A.B., J.C.D., The Banns of Marriage, XIV-140 pp., 1931.

65. Ryder, Rev. Raymond Aloysius, A.B., J.C.D., Simony, IX-151 pp., 1931.
66. Campagna, Rev. Angelo, Ph.D., J.U.D., Il Vicario Generale del Vescovo, VII-205 pp., 1931.
67. Cox, Rev. Joseph Godfrey, A.B., J.C.D., The Administration of Seminaries, VI-124 pp., 1931.
68. Gregory, Rev. Donald J., J.U.D., The Pauline Privilege, XV-165 pp., 1931.
60. Donohue, Rev. John F., J.C.D., The Impediment of Crime, VIII-110 pp., 1931.
70. Dooley, Rev. Eugene A., O.M.I., J.C.D., Church Law on Sacred Relics, IX-143 pp., 1931.
71. Orth, Rev. Clement Raymond, O.M.C., J.C.D., The Approbation of Religious Institutes, 171 pp., 1931.
72. Pernicone, Rev. Joseph M., A.B., J.C.D., The Ecclesiastical Prohibition of Books, XII-267 pp., 1932.
73. Clinton, Rev. Connell, A.B., J.C.D., The Paschal Precept, IX-108 pp., 1932.
74. Donnelly, Rev. Francis B., A.M., S.T.L., J.C.D., The Diocesan Synod, VIII-125 pp., 1932
75. Torrente, Rev. Camilo, C.M.F., J.C.D., Las Processiones Sagradas, V-145 pp., 1932.
76. Murphy, Rev. Edwin J., C.PP.S., J.C.D., Suspension Ex Informata Conscientia, XI-122 pp., 1932.
77. MacKenzie, Rev. Eric F., A.M., S.T.L., J.C.D., The Delict of Heresy in its Commission, Penalization, Absolution, VII-124 pp., 1932.
78. Lyons, Rev. Avitus E., S.T.B., J.C.D., The Collegiate Tribunal of First Instance, XI-147 pp., 1932.
79. Connolly, Rev. Thomas A., J.C.D., Appeals, XI-195 pp., 1932.
80. Sangmeister, Rev. Joseph V., A.B., J.C.D., Force and Fear as Precluding Matrimonial Consent, V-211 pp., 1932.
81. Jaeger, Rev. Leo A., A.B., J.C.D., The Administration of Vacant and Quasi-Vacant Episcopal Sees in the United States, IX-229 pp. 1932.
82. Rimlinger, Rev. Herbert T., J.C.D., Error Invalidating Matrimonial Consent, VII-79 pp., 1932.
83. Barrett, Rev. John D. M., S.S., J.C.D., Comparative Study of the Third Plenary Council and the Code, IX-221 pp., 1932.
84. Carberry, Rev. John J., Ph.D., S.T.D., J.C.L., The Juridical Form of Marriage, 1934.
85. Dolan, Rev. John L., A.B., J.C.L., The Defensor Vinculi, 1934.
86. Hannan, Rev. Jerome D., A.M., S.T.D., LL.B., J.C.L., The Canon Law of Wills, 1934.
87. Lemieux, Rev. Delisle A., A.M., J.C.L., The Sentence in Ecclesiastical Procedure, 1934.
88. O'Rourke, Rev. James J., A.B., J.C.L., Parish Registers, 1934.

89. Timlin, Rev. Bartholomew, O.F.M., A.M., J.C.L., Conditional Matrimonial Consent, 1934.
90. Wahl, Rev. Francis X., A.B., J.C.L., The Matrimonial Impediments of Consanguinity and Affinity, 1934.
91. White, Rev. Robert J., A.B., LL.B., S.T.B., J.C.L., Canonical Ante-Nuptial Promises and the Civil Law, 1934.

www.ingramcontent.com/pod-product-compliance
Lightning Source LLC
LaVergne TN
LVHW050227080826
844660LV00012B/485